PARANORMAL MAGAZINE SET

(Issue 1, 2, 3)

THE GHOST HUNTERS MAG

STEAMPUNKED

INTRODUCTION

-

The world of paranormal at your figure tips, in a unique style Magazine book

Features:
Famous Paranormal Cases
New Hauntings
Retro analysis on old Ghost Pictures
Funky paranormal equipment's
A to Z Series
Make your Own

Plus much more..

In the theme of STEAMPUNK, with recreational illustrations

Just how educated are we on the paranormal, we plan to learn and amaze with you with the most best kept secrets in the paranormal community.

**LEE STEER
AUTHOR – EDITOR**

**SIMON MILLER
HISTORIAN AUTHOR**

**WAYNE RIDSDEL
AUTHOR –
ILLUSTRATOR**

CONTENTS

-

A TO Z'S
A B C

FAMOUS PARANORMAL CASES
BORLEY RECTORY
PONTERFRACT POLTERGEIST

GHOST HUNTERS GUIDE
PART ONE

PARANORMAL EQUIPMENT
VAN DER GRAAF
MAKE AN EM PUMP

NEW HAUNTINGS

OLD TRADITIONS

A TO Z'S
BY SIMON MILLER

APPARITION

This is the term used by professional ghost researchers to describe all kinds of ghosts no matter whether they are human, animal or objects.

So how can we improve our chances of seeing an apparition?

Don your Geist goggles and let's look for some.

Using the latest infrared and full spectrum technology will help us see what the naked eye cannot

BHOOT/ BHUT (INDIAN FOLKLORE)

The restless ghost of a deceased person, usually appearing in human form but with backward-facing feet. Bhoots tend to appear in white, often floating above the ground or in trees, and cast no shadow.

In many regions, bhoots are supposed to fear water and steel or iron objects, so keeping those nearby is believed to scare them off also the scent of burnt turmeric is also said to ward them off. So while hunting ghosts in The Jewel of the Crown make sure you have the right equipment to hand.

CIHUATETEO (AZTEC MYTHOLOGY)

The ancient Aztecs regarded childbirth as a form of battle, so women who died giving birth were honored as fallen warriors. In death, they became the fearsome Cihuateteo, known for haunting crossroads, causing sickness and madness, and stealing children. Do not get on their bad side.

FAMOUS PARANORMAL CASES

BY WAYNE RIDSDEL

BACK TO BORLEY RECTORY

INTRODUCTION

Many people, from all over the world are quite happy to view and judge the controversial history of Borley Rectory, on evidence compiled and presented by the famous, and it has to be said, equally controversial Harry Price. However, in reality the saga of the once famously named 'most haunted house in England began several centuries before the former stage magician and renowned paranormal researcher entered the arena.

There is no denying that Harry Price was ultimately responsible for bringing an often unwelcomed storm of public interest down on the quiet, rural Sussex/Essex border village of Borley. It is also worth noting that other reputable individuals investigated this location during the time of Price's eventful investigation period of 1926 - 1939. And countless other researchers subsequently followed on after Borley Rectory burned to the ground in 1939, and Prices death on March 29th 1948. All research following these dates have either been on examination of public historical records, personal testament from contemporary witnesses, or retrospective analysis of the limited experiences and documents Harry Price deemed to make public.

While I have made every possible effort to ensure that the facts in this article are obtained from credible and reliable sources, I make no attempt to change the reader's opinions or influence anyone one way or the other. My main goal is to briefly set out available information to help the reader form their own subsequent course of research and verification, and of course to make interesting reading about an intriguing chain of events that has permanently etched itself into the annals of paranormal research.

TRACING THE ORIGINS

Before we can consider the credibility of any reported or experienced phenomena in any investigation it is essential to pay particular attention to their possible cause or origins. As an example of this, let me highlight one of, if not *the* most famous incidents of the Borley Rectory nun. By carrying out meticulous research of historical records, and considering local folklore, strong evidence emerged that the ***apparition*** of the nun reported to have walk forlornly around Borley Rectory grounds, could in fact be linked to a 13th century nun, who it is said was discovered while attempt to elope with a young monk from the monastery that once stood on the Rectory site. As a consequence of this strictly forbidden affair, the monk was quickly executed and the nun, (documented in historical records as one 'Marie Lairre'), was bricked up alive in an undisclosed wall of the former monastery. Although at first glance this tragic event sounds conveniently plausible, further detailed research was to show that the nearby convent that the nun is alleged to have been a resident, never existed.

Despite this obvious missing link causing doubt in an age-old explanation of events, it appears to be constantly and conveniently ignored, thus a false account of true events still fuels local folklore and academic research to this day, and the centuries-old legend of the Borley Rectory nun continues to entertain and astound subsequent generations of paranormal enthusiasts.

I make no apology for further mention of the Borley Rectory nun in later sections of this article, she is a key aspect of the Borley Rectory phenomena and any retrospective analysis of the location and relevant characters would not be complete, nor indeed accurate without her inclusion.

THE BULL YEARS

Following the death of Rev. John Phillip Herringham in 1862, the Rev. Henry Dawson Ellis Bull took up the residency of Borley Manor; a small 17th century house, complete with tithe barn, located beside the church, and still stands today.

It was not long however, before the new Rector and his family out grew this modest abode and Henry Bull decided to have a new home built on a nearby site that had been the site of a previous rectory building. In 1863, the new and larger rectory was completed, at an estimated cost of £3,000.

There is still much speculation as to why the previous Rector of Borley had elected to live in the small Borley Manor House, instead of the much larger and more commodious dwelling that Henry Bull saw fit to replace. Many subsequent researchers of the Borley Mystery believe, the old rectory house may have been possessed by similar phenomena to its larger and more famous replacement, and had troubled the Herringham family enough for them to desert the place and seek alternative accommodation.

Over the years that followed Borley Rectory was to be improved and extended, reaching its final state of completion between the years of 1875 and 1892.

Very quickly after the Bull family moved into their new home the legendary phenomena that was to plague Borley Rectory for many decades began and gradually escalated until the Bull occupancy ended in 1927.

It has to be noted that of all the occupants of this sprawling, and some would call it, 'a ugly building'; the Bull's were not only the least distressed by the strange events that occurred on an unprecedented scale, they actually seemed to relish in them, making them an entertaining part of their everyday life. It became common and popular practice for Rev. Henry D.E. Bull to indulge his 14 children with chilling ghost stories, many of his own invention throughout the dark, cold winter nights. Maybe this complacency was the reason for the family's acceptance of the phenomena that was to follow.

Let me now try to highlight some of the afore-mentioned phenomena in the hope that the reader can draw their own conclusions:

One of the earliest incidents which occurred at Borley Rectory, under the Bull occupancy, in fact, not long after the Bull family moved in, involved two of the young Bull sisters. While out in the garden, accompanied by the family's maid, and looking out over the surrounding countryside from the gateway; the two sisters noticed two of their friends approaching. They were curious, however, about a third young girl, dressed in white summery clothes, walking a short distance in front, (some accounts say the girl was dressed in pale blue).

At first glance, one would be forgiven for thinking that this incident is hardly unusual, let alone paranormal in any way. That is, until we learn that when the two Bull sisters asked their two friends about the identity of their friend, the two friends denied all knowledge of a third party being anywhere in sight.

Although this bizarre incident raised little alarm or interest at the time, a girl matching the same description does appear on several more occasions in the subsequent years; for example, there is an unsubstantiated claim of the sighting of a young girl hanging desperately from the window sill of the famous Blue Room window, before crashing with fatal results through the glass roof of the conservatory below. Then again, a young girl matching the same description was seen by several onlookers, as she stood looking out from the Blue Room window on the night Borley Rectory burnt to the ground in 1939. Strangely, at the time of this incident, the fire had already devastated the build and the entire floor between the two levels of the house had been completely destroyed, and no longer existed.

Another strange and frequently occurring phenomena during this period was the annoying ringing of the servants bells. Even when there were no persons about to activate them, the servants bells would ring regularly and often persistently. Many explanations have been offered for this bizarre phenomena over the years. For example, in their book: 'The Haunting of Borley Rectory', E.J. Dingwall, K.M. Goldney and T.H. Hall, suggest that the bell ringing phenomena was a result of mice or rats getting among the rafters and interfering with the bell wires. This explanation may seem plausible, until one considers the fact that the bells continued to ring, long after the bell wires had been removed to eliminate this annoying problem.

Albeit few and far between, there are documented accounts of actual physical assault taking place during alleged poltergeist incidents. Again, these seemed to predominantly revolve around the Bull sisters, in particular, Ethel, the eldest. On one such incident, Ethel had been lying fast asleep in bed, when she was cruelly and abruptly awoken by a vicious slap about her face from an unseen hand.

The then young Ethel Bull was the victim of another distressing phenomena. Each night as she retired to bed, she would fall victim to long sessions of loud, rapping noises on her bedroom door, followed by loud bangs and crashes throughout the house.

The most persistent and long-lasting feature to plague Borley Rectory, right from the time of its construction to the time of its demolition in the latter months of World war Two, was undoubtedly the sound of heavy footsteps, heard throughout the entire house, usually emanating from parts of the house where no one was present.

Documents and witness statements show that during the Bull sisters childhood years all the girls would hear footsteps passing their bedroom doors, moving along the landing, until finally stopping outside the night nursery. When the footsteps stopped, three loud raps would be heard and then all would fall silent.

The Bull sisters were not the only witnesses of these strange footsteps. All the Bull family members, and all the subsequent families and their guests all testified to hearing them at some point during the Rectories mysterious history. Many guests became so unnerved by this particular phenomena over the years and as a consequence refused to sleep in the house again.

Another mystery that presented itself regularly concerned the appearance of lights in parts of the house known not to have been in use. Just like the aforementioned phenomena, the strange and inexplicable appearance of lights was reported by several people throughout the Rectories illustrious existence. It is worth noting at this stage that at no point during its history did Borley Rectory possess gas or electric, any illumination was provided exclusively by oil lamps.

Now let us examine some of the phenomena witnessed by other Bull family members and their respective quests. We'll begin with Harry Bull and his close friend and fellow student, at Wadham College, Oxford at the time in question. Shaw Jeffrey spent at least one, maybe two summer vacations at Borley Rectory. I should however, point out to the reader that the account of Shaw Jeffrey's stay at Borley Rectory was recounted and documented many years later when had become an old man, and admits he was unable to recall the exact years in which these incidents took place, however, the content of his curious incidents is described by with surprising detail and clarity. This fact alone suggests that whatever the young Shaw Jeffrey experienced it was enough to etch itself clearly into his memory throughout his remaining life.

He recalls: on several occasions seeing stones falling about inside the house. The sound of a horse-drawn carriage and most interestingly of all, while in the company of various Bull family members, (not just the sisters), he is one of the Borley Rectory guests who claim to have seen the apparition of the mysterious nun on more than one occasion.

The sound of footsteps was not restricted to inside the house. Several witnesses claim to have heard them on the road outside. One witness in particular experienced this phenomena. Harry Bull's brother, Walter, who spent much of his life at sea, testifies that when visiting Borley Rectory, he was aware of someone following close behind him on at least fifty occasions, but was never able to see anyone present at the time.

There are some accounts on record where these mysterious footsteps actually manifested into a much more distressing experience, one incident was described by the unfortunate Ethel Bull, after falling victim to it whilst walking along one of the long, dark corridors on the upper floor, late one night.

She heard the familiar footsteps and suddenly became aware of someone standing next to her. She turned and to her absolute horror, saw a tall, dark complexioned man only inches away from her. Before poor Ethel could compose herself, the man completely vanished.

On another occasion, this time after she had retired to bed for the night, Ethel was suddenly awoken and found a strange looking man standing beside her bed. The stranger was wearing a tall hat and was dressed in very old-fashioned costume. It seems, however, that Ethel was not the only person to suffer this strange nocturnal visitors attentions. Ethel's sister, Freda, reports several times of being visited in the night by this strange apparition and finding him either standing by, or sitting on her bed, after being abruptly awoken.

Another Bull family member who experienced many paranormal incidents was the Reverend Henry Foyster Bull, (more popularly known as 'Harry'). It has to be said, however, that over the years, Harry's experiences have received, by far the most scepticism, and Harry himself has been dismissed by many sceptics as a 'teller of tall tales'. However, no analysis of Borley Rectory mysteries would be complete, or indeed accurate without including the alleged phenomena witnessed by the original Rector's son, Harry.

Harry inherited the post of Rector of Borley in 1827 and carried out these duties until his death in 1927. It is important to note that Harry did not reside in Borley Rectory itself for this entire period. For many years he and his wife took up residence in nearby Borley Place, where he was born. His motivation for his choice of accommodation was the more amenable comfort and more up-to-date facilities within Borley Place, and not any desire or need to escape the unwelcomed effects caused by the phenomena that plagued the much larger, but less hospitable Rectory building.

One of the most frequently reported, though sadly unverified incidents experienced by Harry Bull, occurred one day while walking his pet Labrador 'Juvenal' in the extensive gardens of Borley Rectory.

Until the day of this incident 'Juvenal' had always been known to be a calm and confident dog; on the day in question, that was to change. While out in the garden, during the hours of daylight 'Juvenal' began to howl as he stopped and starred at something in the dark shadows among the dense shrubbery. Harry followed his dog's frightened stare, and noticed the legs and feet of someone standing in semi-concealment. What followed next horrified both dog and owner. The legs emerged into the open, and the strange figure appeared to be headless.

Once out in the open, the figure moved directly towards one of the gates, where upon it passed straight through, despite the fact that the gate was not only closed but securely locked. It then completely vanished without trace into the vegetable garden which lay beyond.

It is hardly surprising that the validity of this incident has been contested over the intervening years, and of Harry Price's recording of it. More recently, the incident was investigated again, or at least, a detailed study of Harry Price's notes on the incident were made and re-examined by Robert J. Hastings, a reputable author and paranormal investigator. Price's notes read as follows:

"Harry Bull in the garden one day with the retriever 'Juvenal', who howled and cowered when Bull saw the legs of a man otherwise hidden by fruit trees, pass towards a small postern gate, which was kept locked, and pass through it. Someone chased the headless man through the garden who eventually disappeared in the veg garden."

The description above of this bizarre event was only the first recorded. Several years later in 1929, Mary Pearson, the Reverend Guy Smith's maid claimed that she chased a headless figure across the lawn until it vanished into the surrounding undergrowth.

Again, in 1938/39 Captain Gregson, the final occupant of Borley Rectory, before its demise by fire, lost two of his treasured dogs. During a walk in the grounds, something they stumbled upon in the courtyard frightened the dogs so much, they yelped and ran off, never to be seen again. Captain Gregson, however, reported that he saw nothing untoward and couldn't explain his usually well trained and obedient dogs uncharacteristic behavior.

There is another apparition who is reported by many witnesses to have frequented the grounds of Borley Rectory. Not all together surprisingly, Harry Bull appears to have been one of those witnesses. The apparition in question is that of a little old man. Although seen predominantly around the lawn area, he has been observed in various other locations within the boundaries of Borley Rectory's garden.

If the background research of this discarnate character is to be believed there is a good reason for his favoured choice of appearances. Many Bull family members, (Harry Included), were convinced that it was indeed 'Amos' the old family gardener appearing before them.

Over the years there have been all manner of strange and bizarre sightings in and around Borley Rectory. One such instance that ranks high on this long list, for both frequency and popularity is that of the sight and sound of an old-fashioned horse drawn carriage.

Though this mysterious carriage has been witnessed many times, its description seems to be uncertain. Some say it is black, shiny, illuminated by bright, oil lamps and very ornate in its appearance, others say it is dull and lack-luster, unlit and primitive in its design. The number and appearance of the horses that pull it along the narrow country lanes outside Borley Rectory (usually at alarming speed), also seems to vary according to individual witnesses. Sometimes there are four horses, (black bays), or on other occasions the horses number six, and are said to be pure white.

Maybe the most bizarre and alarming features of this mysterious bygone conveyance are the facts that sometimes the driver appears to be headless, or again, equally strange, some terrified witnesses have claimed that the horses, regardless of their colour and number were also devoid of their heads.

In the next issue we examine some of the claims of Borley Rectory's most infamous haunting phenomena, that of the nun, who regularly wanders forlornly along the 'Nun's Walk' and lonely dark country lanes that lead too and fro from this, probably, most haunted rural location.

THE BLACK MONK OF PONTEFRACT

WAYNE RIDSDEL

In 1966, the Pritchard family, of 30 East Drive, Chequerfield Estate, Pontefract, became the helpless victims of a terrifying chain of events that was to develop into the most unique and violent case of poltergeist activity in the documented history of the paranormal world.

It all began on the evening of 1st September, 1966; this was the time when Joe and Jean Pritchard had recently moved into the house and had decided to take a long – awaited holiday, taking their twelve-year-old daughter, Diane with them.

After much discussion and long heated debates, Joe and Jean reluctantly decided that, due to unresolved, long standing family issues, it would be better for all concerned if their fifteen-year-old son, Phillip, was to stay at home under the watchful supervision of his grandmother, Mrs Sarah Scholes.

After the Pritchards had loaded the car and departed on holiday Sarah Scholes and her grandson settled down for the evening in the living room. Mrs. Scholes occupied herself with her usual past-time of knitting, while Phillip turned on the TV for a night of viewing; although it wasn't long before he had convinced his grandmother to allow him to go visit his friend who lived a few doors away on the same street.

At 9pm. Phillip returned home, as had been stipulated by his grandmother. No sooner had the fifteen-year-old entered the house than a gust of wind blasted through the house and the back door slammed shut. Immediately the living room felt icy cold. Understandably the two of them looked at each other in shock; each of them believing that the back door had mistakenly been left open and when Phillip entered the house through the front door it had resulted in a 'through draft' rushing through the downstairs rooms of the house and quickly dissipating the heat from the gas fire, making the living room instantly feel cold.

However, what happened next could not be explained away quite so easily. It was Phillip who was first to notice that a thick cloud of fine, white dust had begun to descend in the room. Gradually, the dust settled, covering the floor and furniture. Niether of them were frightened at this point, just puzzled. To add to their confusion, it appeared that the strange chalk-like dust was not coming from the ceiling, as only the lower part of the room was being coated.

It was later that same night that events took a turn towards the more decidedly sinister in their nature, which as a result left both Phillip and his terrified grandmother in little doubt that the house they were living in showed all the classic signs of being haunted.

After witnessing a heavy double wardrobe in one of the bedrooms begin to sway from left to right repeatedly and then move across the floor, apparently of its volition; Mrs. Scholes hastily pack a couple of over-night bags and the two of them went to stay at Jean Pritchard's sister's house directly across the road.

Once Mrs. Scholes and Phillip relayed their experience, Marie and her husband Vic took it upon themselves to contact one of their friends, who had often voiced an interest in ghosts and all things paranormal. Mr. O'Donald agreed to come over straight away and investigate the situation.

As soon as Marie, Vic and Mr. O'Donald entered through the front door, a cold blast of air hit them full in the face. Unfortunately nothing else happened while Mr. O'Donald was there, though he did say that a poltergeist might be responsible for the nights events, adding, quite ironically, as it turned out that, poltergeists often damaged photographs.

As the hour was late, Mr. O'Donald went home. However, minutes after he had left, Vic and Marie heard something crash. Upon checking the living room they found the Pritchard's wedding photo on the floor. The glass was smashed and the photo itself was ripped in two.

The events of that night marked the end of the first stage of poltergeist activity. Nothing else unusual happened in the Pritchard family home for two whole years. By the time Joe, Jean and daughter, Diane Pritchard returned from holiday everything had reverted to normal.

After a two year, uneventful break the poltergeist activity returned with vengeance. From the beginning it was clear that the second stage of this horrifying chain of events would be far worse than that of two years previously.

It was late afternoon, when Jean Pritchard and Mrs. Scholes were having tea and they were disturbed by a noise in the hall. When they rushed to investigate they discovered the bed covers from Jean's bed, lying in an untidy heap at the foot of the stairs. Phillip's bedding had also been thrown down the stairs, along with a selection of potted plants that had been on the landing.

Mrs. Scholes stared at the mess then, turned to her daughter and sadly announced, "I told you … It's happening again!"

Over the following days and weeks the occurrence of events increased and worsened in their nature. The whole house was filled with banging noises and thumps. The rooms would turn intensely cold and countless objects began to move around by themselves.

One room in particular was to become the centre of attention in the early days of this second stage of activity. This room was one being decorated by Jean Pritchard. She was horrified one day while she toiled away, when several paintbrushes, a carpet sweeper and a roll of wallpaper was hurled through the air. Some of the objects struck Jean painfully about her body before she could make a hasty and understandably panicked exit from the room.

The kitchen was the next room to be affected, arguably to an even worse degree than the bedroom. Enormous bite marks appeared in a sandwich in the refrigerator.

While the incidents increased in both frequency and severity, the Pritchards decided that they had had enough and took the drastic step of contacting a priest and asking him to perform an exorcism.

The priest did arrive at the house, however, instead of performing the exorcism that the Pritchards requested, he quickly informed them that the disturbing events they had experienced were not the result of poltergeist activity, but, in fact were caused by the house subsiding. This assumption was quickly dismissed when a rather heavy candlestick rose into the air and waved itself from side to side, only inches away from the priest's nose, upon which he hurried from the house proclaiming quite loudly that there was evil within the house.

In this, the second stage of poltergeist activity, the focus of attention semed to have changed from Phillip to Diane, who was now fourteen-years old. On one occasion, she was thrown from her bed during the night, and on another devastating incident, she was dragged upstairs by an apparent pair of invisible hands, which seemed to grab her cardigan.

Eventually another family member came to stay in the house; Joe Pritchard's sister, who was openly sceptical of the entire affair. She made no attempt to hide the fact that she strongly believed that both Diane and Phillip were playing tricks and faking the whole thing to get attention. She was convinced that by her staying in the house, she could prove that her firmly held suspicion was well founded.

No sooner had Aunt Maude set foot in the house the activity appeared to escalate. First of all, to everyone's horror the refrigerator door opened and a jug of milk floated through the air in the kitchen, and poured itself over Maude's head. Even after that bizarre and alarming, she still remained firm in her belief that it was all a trick.

That night, Aunt Maude and Jean arranged to sleep in the same bedroom as Diane, their intention clearly to closely observe her.

Despite the fact that Diane was not left alone all through the night, the poltergeist put on its most impressive performance so far. Food from the refrigerator was strewn all over the kitchen floor. All through the house the lights flickered on and off, and worst of all, when Aunt Maude climbed into bed, the lamp from the bedside cabinet unplugged itself from the wall socket and sailed out of the bedroom door. Finally, at least where than particular night was concerned, four small light bulbs from the gas fire in the living room suddenly appeared in Diane's bedroom.

Ironically, even though Aunt Maude was the most sceptical of all those who were involved in the events that took place in the Pritchard family home, it was she who experienced, arguably one of the most unnerving incidents:

Aunt Maude and Jean were having a conversation in the living room, when suddenly an enormous hairy hand appeared from behind the door, then almost instantly a second hand with the same scary characteristics appeared around the lower edge of the door.

Fearing that some kind of unimaginable monster was about to enter the room, the two women stared in silent horror. Until, after a few seconds, the higher of the two hands beckoned Maude over to it.

It seems that Aunt Maude's scepticism had quickly turned to understandable horror; "Get away … You're evil!" she eventually screamed, before starting to sing hymns, in the hope of frightening whatever the intruder was away.

It was obvious however, that her plan had failed miserably when in response the hands emerged into the room, at which point the two women realised that what they believed to be some kind of horrid monster, was in fact Aunt Maude's very large and very furry gloves. However, the incident was still scary enough to hold both women rigid with fear, when the gloves began beating time and animating themselves in front of Aunt Maude's face, as if they were conducting her hymn singing.

Until now, whatever had been causing the disturbances at the Pritchard's home, had remained invisible, this was to change one night, soon after Maude's visit.

Joe and Jean woke one night to see a hooded figure standing in the doorway of their doorway of their bedroom. When they switched on the lights it vanished. It later transpired that several of Joe and Jen's friends had also seen the hooded figure on other occasions. One witness even stated that she had felt the terrifying figure touch her head.

It was later revealed during subsequent research on this amazing case that a monastery had once been located near the site of number 30 East Drive. Could this hooded figure be the ghost of a former monk who resided at this monastery.

Not long after the night of it's appearance in the bedroom doorway, Diane and Phillip were watching TV when they saw the figure again, this time through the glass of the kitchen door.

Both of them ran after it and entered the kitchen, just in time to see it disappear into the kitchen floor. That was the last time anyone saw or heard of the alleged 'Black Monk of Pontefract.'

Was the Pontefract Poltergeist a hoax? The ghost hunters who investigated the case didn't think so. One of the most famous and respected paranormal investigators of the time, Colin Wilson, said there were too many witnesses and unexplained events that the case only convinced him that ghosts really do exist.

In part two of this article we will take a look at the results of an exclusive investigation carried out by Project Reveal, carried out this year at this famous address. Will the team find any evidence, almost 40 years after the original event to suggest whether the Pontefract Poltergeist was a hoax, or will they unveil evidence of a genuine haunting. You the reader will have exclusive access to information disclosed by Project Reveal's investigation team, after using the latest electronic investigation equipment.

Will their finding compliment this classic poltergeist haunting case from the 1960's or will the use of modern technology and modern investigation techniques back up the suggestion that the whole affair was a hoax designed and executed by the Pritchard family members to gain attention.

All will be revealed in ISSUE 2 of this magazine.

GHOST HUNTING GUIDE AND QUESTIONS

Welcome to the first edition of this Paranormal Magazine. The Editor has asked me as Head of an Investigation team to inspire others and help by giving advice to others. So here is   .

MY STORY

In 2009 I was sitting im my friends car and we were having a discussion on Most Haunted and how there was always activity on every show, and how Ghost Hunter's in the US make their shows and sometimes nothing happens, so we were unsure on which shows to believe and what shows not to believe. So i suggested that we should set up a Paranormal Team and try to find out if those experiences on those shows were actually happening in real life.
Me and my friend Tara worked on some names for the Paranormal team and we decided to come up with South Essex Paranormal Investigation Team, once we had a name i thought it was about time we had a website to promote the team.
There are many sites online that allow you to build your own web page but none i found so useful as the one i have now, I started to build the website with the help of Tara and a famous Social Networking Site, it was soon after that we managed to get our first Private Home Investigation, So we rapidly brought a few bits of equipment from an online shopping site and went to a wholesaler's for a CCTV system. From there we just kept on buying new and better investigation equipment.
After the first investigation we decided that we needed better and bigger toys to do investigations with and that we should hold a few events, So what i done was booked with a few ghost hunting companies to see how they run their events, So off i went to places like The Ragged School in London and The Maltings amongst a few and found that running some of these events was not to hard....boy was i wrong.
It was also quite expensive too.
After looking for at lots of locations we finally found Fort Horsted in Chatham Kent and we decided to book our first event there as they wanted paying after the event so we were quite lucky to find a location that still did that as many wanted money up front that quite

frankly we didnt have being a new and small group just starting out.
We also went to Medium Nights and made friends with lots of
Mediums and we started putting on medium nights on to help pay for
the equipment, Being in Essex (The most Haunted county in the
country) we had many haunted small villages so we thought about
putting on ghost walks on also so give our followers the best of
information that was accurate instead of all those hearsay stories.
We started to get more and more private investigations come in for
our local area and we got to work with other Paranormal groups in
Essex some of them good some of them not so good and soon found
out there is a lot of back stabbing that goes on between teams, We
have always tried not to do that as we are all looking for the same
thing we should work together, that way we have made lots of new
friends.
Everything we do we do with morals and respect it does go a long
way.
Its good to have a set of morals to run your group by.
Now we have gone from strength to strength, We have secured a
venue all for ourselves and we are working on gaining another 2, one
of which is in Canewdon one of the most haunted and famous
churches in Essex. We are the only team that has ever been given
permission to get into the church and the Vicar has even agreed to
give us a talk about the history. So we are very excited about that,
We have got many new locations becoming available for the end of
the year and for 2014. If anyone wants to check out our website feel
free to and leave a comment on the contacts page by going to
www.southessexparanormal.com .

That is really the birth of South Essex Paranormal so if there is
anyone that wants help or advice in setting up a team, or have
already set one up and want some advice please write into us at
southessexparanormal@live.co.uk and we will reply to you. Also
your questions and the answers will appear in the next edition of this
magazine.

IS IT A GHOST

The First picture this issue, is sent from Anita,
Here is what she had to say!

Just curious if anyone else sees anything in the window to the left of the door in
this picture, this photo was taken in the early evening one night after work.
Whenever possible we try to get in a hike.

Seemingly uninhabited house at the base of a hiking trail in Plattsburgh NY

EQUIPMENT

VAN DER GRAAF GENERATOR

Here we have a rather unusual looking machine, called the Van Der Graaf Generator which was Developed in 1929 by Physicist Robert J Van Der Graaf. Now days this device is normally used in schools for education of energy.

This device produces Electro static, from the rotating belt nylon belt, and collects the electric charge within the hollow metal dome, If Touched it would give a nasty shock. nothing life threatening though.

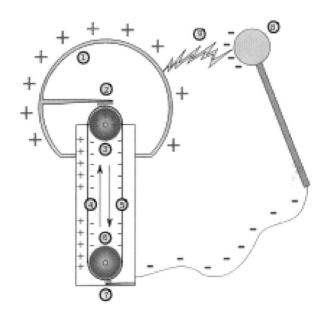

So why would you use this device?
This device creates a positive charge, which has a negative effect on the human body, making you feel like your been touched, could maybe even make you see things which aren't there if you spent to much time within the field,
There is a theory that ghosts are made up of Electrostatic, or need electrostatic to do something or show them self's, This device could be used to test the theory's, by flooding a room with electro static, giving the spirits some energy to play with.
I have not yet to date seen a real scientific controlled experiment with this device and the paranormal field. We would love to hear about your experiments if you try this out!

HOW TO MAKE AN EM PUMP

An EM pump is a mega downgrade to the van der graaf, but it is very similar. The device will emit EMF fields, within a small proximity of the device, So this would affect your k2 meters, and other emf meters. Groups sell these for around £20.00 - £60.00 and they cost less than £5 to make.

Item you need
1 x project box
1 x 9v Motor
1x Earth Magnets "known as rare earth magnets which have an hole in the middle"
1x 9v battery clip
1x Glue

First you will need to glue the rare earth magnet to the end of the 9v motor, (so one side of the magnet is touching the metal pivot of the motor)
Clue Motor to the project box base.
Thread the 9v battery clip through some holes in the project-box and connect to the 9V motor,

Connect the battery and you have a EM pump.

THE GHOSTS OF CHESTERFIELD COLLEGE.

Looking at Chesterfield College from the outside its austere functional 20th century lines would not lead one to believe that you were looking at fertile territory for ghost stories. However, in this you would be wrong. Over the years there have been three deaths on the premises, tragically including a suicide and West block has a history that can be traced back to the late 16th century.

I will start my story with my own particular experiences though I emphasise that I make no claims for supernatural origin and merely present the facts as I experienced them for you to draw your own conclusions.

I started work as a very green biology technician on the 17th of August 1981 and the following occurred late in the afternoon of the day we closed for Christmas (most likely the day before Christmas Eve). In the then laboratory in S233 we kept a large fish tank of Guppies and for this reason we also had a tubifex worm culture to provide live food for them. Over the close down we provided a solid block of food that would slowly dissolve and keep the fish fed but before we went home Ann the senior technician asked me to fetch a beaker of worms to give them a last treat.

The worm culture was located on the old stone slab benches in the glass partitioned balance room at the back of the old S208. These had originally been built to put the accurate mechanical balances on that measure to 10,000[th] of a gramme, to do this they needed to be free of even the slightest vibration. By this time they had been made obsolete by electronic self-leveling balances so the room was used as a store and the slabs made a cool place for the worm culture. Now to appreciate what I'm about to tell, you need to understand the layout of the lab and the prep room. S208 was an old, oak paneled laboratory with gothic looking oak fume cupboards up one side with another in the front corner. Up the center were four huge fixed benches twelve by 5 feet with two inch thick Burma teak tops. Looking to the front of the room the lecturing bench sat atop a dais with the blackboard behind, to the right of this was the door to the prep room and chemical store. To the left of the dais was the door to the main corridor, as already mentioned at the rear of the room was an oak and glass partitioned balance room. The prep room ran the full width of the room and had its own separate door to the main corridor. The one main problem as we shall see was that the laboratory only had light switches by the door to the corridor.

I entered the prep room and walked through into the lab, as I had no wish to go blundering around tripping over stools with a glass beaker in my hand I decided that there was enough light from the windows to make my way down the side to the balance room. I've always had good night vision and this was done fairly easily even though at nearly 4.30 it was totally dark outside there was sufficient light from lampposts to allow me to see, this and a shaft of light from the prep room. I unlocked the door to the balance room, took the lid off the culture, lifted the slice of bread left for the worms to feed on and proceeded to scoop out the tiny little white worms. Whilst doing this I heard someone enter the prep room and noted that they had an exceptionally heavy tread, you could feel the vibrations even at this distance. Then an elderly gentleman entered, he was fairly short, around five feet two or so but exceptionally broadly built almost giving the impression of being square. The other notable thing apart from his heavy tread was the fact he wore a bobble hat. I looked out of the door and called a greeting, not wanting to startle him in the dark but he ignored me and went along setting the fume cupboard doors to the same level (about four inches from closed). I assumed he hadn't heard me or was slightly deaf as he went out again without acknowledging me at all. And that may have been it, after all I was fairly new and there were all kinds of folk I didn't know in such a large college as I been there barely 3 months so I thought no more about it. Some months later a member of the science staff retired and I got talking to another old hand and happened to mention the man I'd seen, assuming he too had retired. He shook his head and said no-one had left recently and asked me to describe the person I'd seen. As I told him what had happened a thoughtful look came to his face and he said "well if I didn't know better I'd say you were describing Charlie". I asked if he'd left recently only for him to say "he died twenty years ago". He went on to say that Charlie was a keen field biologist and walked the peaks at every opportunity and he only owned one pair of footwear, hob nailed walking boots that meant his tread could be heard long before he was seen. It also seemed that Charlie was bald so always wore a bobble hat almost the entire year; he was also short and thickset. Another interesting fact was that for a time he'd actually lived in the prep room when he'd run across hard times. The college was a very different community then and the caretakers and management had turned a blind eye to their unofficial lodger in fact the washing line that he strung across the sink to dry his smalls was still used for drying chromatography papers right up to the refurbishment last summer. So that was my experience of S208.

It turned out that the room had a reputation of being haunted long before my experience Over the years there had been several other incidents so much so that the cleaners always worked in there as a pair rather than alone as normal for the other rooms. One lecturer walking past on their way home after teaching an evening class was startled to see a man walk through the locked door from the darkened lab straight in front of her. On another occasion a curious caretaker locking up one night pressed his face to the window in the door to look into the dark lab that had such a malevolent reputation. Just as his nose touched the pane the door shook as if from a violent blow making the poor fellow jump out of his skin. He decided to beat a hasty retreat.

On another occasion the lab was being used to collate masses of mathematics work books, because of the scale of the job each technician did a turn in strict rota and and my senior technician took her radio to keep her amused while doing this. At the end of the day she returned to our prep room vowing never to go into S208 again, it would seem that when she turned the radio off there was an annoyed harrumph from the prep room and the door slammed violently shut with a resounding bang, even though the room was empty and locked. Sometime later a female technician came to work in chemistry and she frequently talked of hearing Charlie pottering about in the lab next door. She also pointed out that no matter where the fume cupboard doors were set; they were always put to the same four inch height when you came back that I'd seen the man setting them to. However, on one occasion her happy acceptance of Charlie was severely tested. She phoned me at the end of the day and asked if I'd come over to the chemistry prep room but would say no more. Mystified I walked round. When I got there I was met on the corridor by an ashen face technician clutching her bag and coat, "can you turn the light off in there" I was asked? When I asked why she merely said "you'll see". Again the light switches in this old part of the college were awkwardly placed as the original building had been lit by gas (there was still a gas mantel in S203 up until recently), and involved walking over to the other side of the room. I turned the switch off and turned to go out as I did so the light came back on, as I reached to turned it off again it went off before I could do so, only to relight as I turned away. The switch itself wasn't moving but I'd had enough and told the technician to go and I'd report it as a wiring fault. Needless to say for narrative tension, no fault could be discovered the next day and the same switch worked perfectly until ripped out last summer.

After this the ducting for the fume cupboards was ripped out, now I don't know if it was the disturbance, noise or whatever but all this seems to have been too much for Charlie who moved out and was never heard of again. My other experience was again on the second floor of south block a few years ago. We'd had a chemical amnesty and had amassed a large volume of waste chemicals for disposal. The firm had arranged for collection early on a Saturday morning and rather than make a special journey over from near Doncaster, Bob tempted me to see to the loading of the wagon with promises of overtime for Christmas. We'd collected trolleys from all over and put the chemicals on these and stored them last thing Friday in S222 to allow easy loading of the goods lift the next morning. The Saturday proved overcast and dull and at 6.00 it was still fairly dark. The caretaker let me in then retired to his office; I had the entire south block to myself. I took the first trolley and stood it in the goods lift door to keep it open whilst I loaded the others. Now if anyone has been in the college when it's dark you'll know what I'm talking about here. On the ground, first and second floors the corridor by the lifts are very long. Sometime you can give yourself a fright by seeing your repeated image in the progression of fire doors along its length, especially if you're wearing a white lab coat. The impression is of a slightly transparent figure walking towards you. As I took out the last trolley I glanced up the corridor only to see this effect. I looked down; embarrassed that I'd fallen for it again, realising that it was only my reflection. It was only when I was pulling the last trolley onto the lift that I realised I wasn't wearing my lab coat. Now with a real touch of the jitters I pressed the lift door close button and with relief watched it slide to, only at the last minute for there to be a beep as if something had been inserted in the way and see the door open again. The high pitched whine continued and door refused to close, now thoroughly un-nerved I peered out into the empty corridor, then I checked the door runner to see if anything was in the way, nothing. A last my temper gave way and I shouted "oh stop ####ing about" immediately at which the beeping stopped, the door Closed and the lift descended.

By now the lorry had arrived and we quickly loaded the various barrels with the chemicals. When I was done I decided nothing would entice me to return to the second floor (not even time and a half) and I'd leave taking the empty trolleys up until Monday.

Other people have also reported seeing ghosts, one cleaner frequently claimed to see a young child wandering the corridors in west block. She said he wore a tall Eton collar and very old fashioned suit.

An ex chief caretaker also saw an old employee early one morning when he'd just unlocked the front door. He walked through reception and into what had been the old engineering labs through a locked door. He said the individual was plainly recognisable, however it was impossible for it to be the person in question as he'd died in rather tragic circumstances a few years earlier.

Over the years there have also been stories relating to odd occurrences on the mezzanine of the library with doors opening and closing without being touched and the sound of footsteps. Several people have also talked of poltergeist like activity in the refectory with items dropping off tables or skimming across the room, this when it was virtually empty.

Also to be borne in mind is the fact that the college owns the lease on Tapton house. Over the years there have been several spectral sightings of George Stephenson. When the building was still used as a school a terrified cleaner was confronted one morning by an old gentleman in a nightshirt emerging from the room at the head of the stairs and demanding in a strong North Eastern accent "where's my hot water?" In the time of the college's tenancy there have been reports of footsteps and opening doors when there was no one else in the building.

Tradition also has it that the ghost of Charles Markham, another tenant of the house has, from time to time, been seen strolling around the grounds cutting and Edwardian dash in his plus fours.

So, when you're going home tonight and you see someone approaching you, just make sure..

Oakland's House is a Victorian house built in 1865/7 for Frederick Wells, a successful coal merchant, timber merchant, brewer and Borough Alderman. It was built in the Italianate style and was probably designed by Charles Pertwee, Frederick Well's brother-in-law. Frederick chose this style after seeing Osborne House, Queen Victoria's residence on the Isle of Wight. The bell tower is typical of this style Oaklands House was one of the largest and most imposing houses in Chelmsford. It is now smaller than originally built as the servant's quarters were demolished between 1920 and 1930.

Oaklands House together with Oaklands Park was purchased by Chelmsford Borough Council in 1929. In 2006, English Heritage recognised the importance of Oaklands House by awarding Grade 2 listed status.

From about 1950 onwards, the emphasis of the collection was changed to concentrate more on Chelmsford and Essex which resulted in foreign material being moved to other museums.

In 1973 a single storey extension was added to exhibit artefacts on loan from the Essex Regiment Trust.

This extension was demolished in 2008 and has been replaced by a larger extension of contrasting design.

So would you like to run your own Paranormal Investigations into this wonderful picturesque Museum and take a look around after dark. South Essex Paranormal are the in house paranormal team. The price for the Museum is £600 this includes free first aid cover at your event. And you can run it how ever you wish. You will have access to all area's of the museum that the general public never see. The times of the events booked can run any time between 7pm till 4am please email southessexparanormal@live.co.uk or call 07812566438 for details

ST MARKS EVE (THE PORCH WATCH)

'Tis now, replied the village belle,
St. Mark's mysterious eve,
And all that old traditions tell
I tremblingly believe;
How, when the midnight signal tolls,
Along the churchyard green,
A mournful train of sentenced souls
In winding-sheets are seen.
The ghosts of all whom death shall doom
Within the coming year,
In pale procession walk the gloom,
Amid the silence drear.'

The Year is 1923 and the Reverend Morris of Newbiggin, Beverley is writing to Harry Price after hearing of him exposing the fake spirit photographer, William Hope.

Dear Mr Price,

I recently read about you exposing the fakir sprit photographer and was hoping you could gleam some light on recent happenings in our village of Newbiggin. A local lady called Mary Morritt has been practicing an old tradition of the porch watch on April the 24th every year, much to my disdain, but without much in the way of nuisance. However for the last 3 years she has been predicting the deaths of certain parishioners to my Warden, all of which have come to pass which i am sure you will understand is unnerving my flock.

The date is coming around again and if she is to use her second sight, call it what you will, i fear that she will be tried for witchcraft or mobbed by the locals. If you could find the time to visit our village around this date we would accommodate your needs and i will supply all the information i have on this Practice accompanying this letter.

Yours Sincerely
Rev M.C.F. Morris B.C.L., M.A

In Shakespeare's A Midsummers Nights Dream, the Bard has Puck say;

Now it is that time of night,
That the graves all gaping wide,
Every one lets forth his sprite,
In the church-way paths to glide

Exert from Chambers Book Of Days:

In the northern parts of England, it is still believed that if a person, on the eve of St. Mark's day, watch in the church porch from eleven at night till one in the morning, he will see the apparitions of all those who are to be buried in the churchyard during the ensuing year. The following illustration of this superstition is found among the Hollis manuscripts, in the Lansdowne Collection. The writer, Gervase Hollis, of Great Grimsby, in Lincolnshire, was a colonel in the service of Charles the First, and by no means one who could be termed a superstitious man, even in his own day. He professes to have received the tale from Mr. Liveman Rampaine, minister of God's word at Great Grimsby, in Lincolnshire, who was household chaplain to Sir Thomas Munson, of Burton, in Lincoln, at the time of the incident.

'In the year 1631, two men (inhabitants of Burton) agreed betwixt themselves upon St. Mark's eve at night to watch in the churchyard at Burton, to try whether or no (according to the ordinary belief amongst the common people) they should see the Spectra, or Phantasma of those persons which should die in that parish the year following. To this intent, having first performed the usual ceremonies and superstitions, late in the night, the moon shining then very bright, they repaired to the church porch, and there seated themselves, continuing there till near twelve of the clock. About which time (growing weary with expectation and partly with fear) they resolved to depart, but were held fast by a kind of insensible violence, not being able to move a foot.

About midnight, upon a sudden (as if the moon had been eclipsed), they were environed with a black darkness; immediately after, a kind of light, as if it had been a resultancy from torches. Then appears, coming towards the church porch, the minister of the place, with a book in his hand, and after him one in a winding-sheet, whom they both knew to resemble one of their neighbours. The church doors immediately fly open, and through pass the apparitions, and then the doors clap to again. Then they seem to hear a muttering, as if it were the burial service, with a rattling of bones and noise of earth, as in the filling up of a grave. Suddenly a still silence, and immediately after the apparition of the curate again, with another of their neighbours following in a winding-sheet, and so a third, fourth, and fifth, every one attended with the same circumstances as the first.

These all having passed away, there ensued a serenity of the sky, the moon shining bright, as at the first; they themselves being restored to their former liberty to walk away, which they did sufficiently affrighted. The next day they kept within doors, and met not together, being both of them exceedingly ill, by reason of the affrightment which had terrified them the night before. Then they conferred their notes, and both of them could very well remember the circumstances of every passage. Three of the apparitions they well knew to resemble three of their neighbours; but the fourth (which seemed an infant), and the fifth (like an old man), they could not conceive any resemblance of. After this they confidently reported to every one what they had done and seen; and in order designed to death those three of their neighbours, which came to pass accordingly.

Shortly after their deaths, a woman in the town was delivered of a child, which died likewise. So that now there wanted but one (the old man), to accomplish their predictions, which likewise came to pass after this manner. In that winter, about mid-January, began a sharp and long frost, during the continuance of which some of Sir John Munson's friends in Cheshire, having some occasion of intercourse with him, despatched away a foot messenger (an ancient man), with letters to him. This man, tramling this bitter weather over the mountains in Derbyshire, was nearly perished with cold, yet at last he arrived at Burton with his letters, where within a day or two he died. And these men, as soon as ever they see him, said peremptorily that he was the man whose apparition they see, and that doubtless he would die before he returned, which accordingly he did.'

It may readily be presumed that this would prove a very pernicious superstition, as a malignant person, bearing an ill-will to any neighbour, had only to say or insinuate that he had seen him forming part of the visionary procession of St. Mark's Eve, in order to visit him with. a serious affliction, if not with mortal disease. Of a similar tendency was a custom indulged in among cottage families on St. Mark's Eve, of riddling out all the ashes on the hearth-stone over night, in the expectation of seeing impressed upon them, in the morning, the footstep of any one of the party who was to die during the ensuing year. In circles much given to superstition, great misery was sometimes created by a malicious or wanton person coming slily into the kitchen during the night, and marking the ashes with the shoe of one of the party.

The Ghost of Eastry Church, Kent 1956

Advertisements

If you would like to advertise in the paranormal magazine, for a very small fee you can.

Please email asteer8@aol.com

If you would like to: Sell Equipment's – Advertise Ghost Hunts – Self Promotions,

Full page - £60.00
Two Pages - £90.00
Half page - £30.00
Paragraph - £20.00

Submitting Articles

If you feel you have a good article to submit to us to show on our next issue FREE OF CHARGE, please email asteer8@aol.com

The Article Should be non-promotional, however we will allow a website URL at the end of your article.

PROJECT-REVEAL

A BIG THANK YOU FOR SUPPORTING US WITH THIS MAGAZINE.

WE HOPE TO SEE YOU AGAIN WITH OUR NEXT ISSUE DUE OUT ON

31ST OCTOBER.

PROJECT-REVEAL

THE PARANORMAL MAGAZINE

VOLUME TWO

LIKE US! ON FACEBOOK

www.facebook.com/theparanormalmagazine

WIN A Signed Copy Of Issue 3

Give an honest REVIEW of our book to win the chance to win a signed copy of issue 3.

Please visit amazon.co.uk or .com to write the review about this book.

LEE STEER
AUTHOR — EDITOR

WAYNE RIDSDEL
ILLUSTRATOR, AUTHOR

THE PARANORMAL MAGAZINE

A Unique Style magazine like no other...
Brought to you from the 2 minds of: Lee Steer, Wayne Ridsdel,
With help from Philip & john Williams

The mission is to Educate, and showcase the world of the
paranormal, Featuring Famous Hauntings, A to Z, Ghost Hunting
Equipment's, How to Makes, Myths and legends, Fakes BUSTED,
Old traditions, Ghost Pictures, New Hauntings, and much more..

Thanks for showing an interest in our official paranormal magazine
series
All enquires please email
Asteer8@aol.com

In this ISSUE you get a free Pendulum Board cutout.

HAPPY HALLOWEEN

CONTENTS

A TO Z
D, E, F

-

SAMHAIN

-

FAMOUS HAUNTINGS
THE COCK LANE POLTERGEIST
BORLEY RECTORY PART 2

-

HALLOWEEN SUPERSTITIONS

-

BLACK EYED PEOPLE

-

BUSTED

-

THE SMETHWICK BATHS HAUNTINGS

-

HALLOWEEN HOW IT SHOULD BE

EQUIPMENT
FRANKS BOX

A TO Z

In each issue we cover 3 letters from the a to z, this issue we will cover
D, E, F.

Demon

Known as a nasty violent spirit, you wouldn't want to come across within
your lifetime. A demon is believed to be a bad angel, rebelled by god.

They love to attach them self to a body "host" making them feel
psychically ill, some cases state that the demon talks through them, also
making them do things they wouldn't normally do.

These nasty spirit beings, are deformed and grotesque, they hate god, and
those who seek god.

Would you dare to face the demon?

Signs of a demon
3 Knocks
Strange animal activity "birds, cat, dogs"
Heavy objects will move, targeting at you or your guests.
Religious objects will disappear or move..
Growling sounds
Activity happens when prayers are said

Ectoplasm

Is believed to be spirit residue, known as a slimy substance which comes from ghosts any avid "ghost buster movie" fan would know.

All joking aside, Ecto is Greek meaning Outside, and Plasma means something formed.

Mainly famous in the years 1800 – 1900 this white/grey/transparent is meant to come out of solid objects, but in most cases it's known to come from a spiritual medium, while conducting a séance

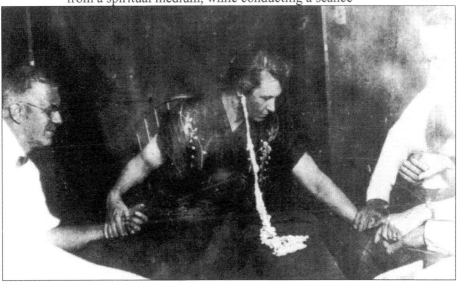

Above picture shows ectoplasm coming from a mediums ear.

Sadly on many occasions the mediums ectoplasm was proven to be fake by a famous investigator harry price! Money desperate people went to great lengths to try and con the public into spirit existence.

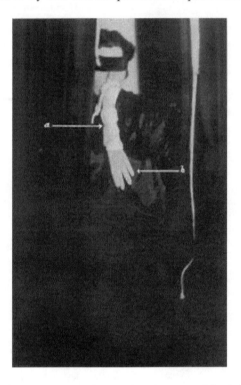

In this picture it was proven that Helen Duncan faked the ectoplasm making out that a spirit arm manifested through her.

This picture was achieved by cheesecloth and a rubber glove.

Was all the séances fake ectoplasm?
Will we ever know?

Full spectrum

How could you possibly see a ghost? Well Full spectrum may be the answer.

A special camera which can see the broad full spectrum of light,
UV – WHITE LIGHT – IR

The majority of cameras you buy in the shops come with a filter fitted under the lens, called a UV filter. Which filters Ultra violet light, UV, and Infrared Light IR.

Removing this filter would enable your camera to see the full spectrum of light; you will notice a slight pink tint to your pictures, this is due to the suns UV rays.

It's a theory that ghosts / spirits may lurk in the different spectrums which we cannot see, and the only way to see into these spectrums is with these modified cameras.

Full Spectrum at night with an IR illuminator

SAMHAIN

Halloween or Samhain was first a ancient, pre-Christian Celtic festival of the dead. The Celtic peoples, who were once found all over Europe, divided the year by four major holidays. According to their calendar, the year began on a day corresponding to November 1st on our present calendar. The date marked the beginning of winter.
Since there was pastoral to the faith , it was a time when cattle and sheep had to be moved to closer pastures and all livestock had to be secured for the winter months. Crops were harvested and stored. The date marked both an ending and a beginning in an eternal cycle.

Samhain (pronounced Sah-ween) It was the biggest and most significant holiday of the Celtic year. The Celts believed that at the time of Samhain, more so than any other time of the year, the ghosts of the dead were able to mingle with the living, because at Samhain the souls of those who had died during the year travelled into the otherworld. People gathered to sacrifice animals, fruits, and vegetables. They also lit bonfires in honour of the dead, to aid them on their journey, and to keep them away from the living. On that day all manner of beings were there such as ghosts, fairies, and demons. To commemorate the event, Druids built huge sacred bonfires, where the people gathered to burn crops and animals as sacrifices to the Celtic deities.

During the celebration, the Celts wore costumes, typically consisting of animal heads and skins, and attempted to tell each other's fortunes. When the celebration was over, they re-lit their hearth fires, which they had extinguished earlier that evening, from the sacred bonfire to help protect them during the coming winter. By A.D. 43, Romans had conquered the majority of Celtic territory. In the course of the four hundred years that they ruled the Celtic lands, two festivals of Roman origin were combined with the traditional Celtic celebration of Samhain. The first was Feralia, a day in late October when the Romans traditionally commemorated the passing of the dead. The second was a day to honour Pomona, the Roman goddess of fruit and trees.

By the 800s, the influence of Christianity had spread into Celtic lands. In the seventh century, Pope Boniface IV designated November 1 All Saints' Day, a time to honor saints and martyrs. It is widely believed today that the pope was attempting to replace the Celtic festival of the dead with a related, but church-sanctioned holiday. The celebration was also called All-hallows or All-Hallowmas (from Middle English Alholowmesse meaning All Saints' Day) and the night before it, the night of Samhain, began to be called All-hallows Eve and, eventually, Halloween. Even later, in A.D. 1000, the church would make November 2 All Souls' Day, a day to honour the dead. It was celebrated similarly to Samhain, with big bonfires, parades, and dressing up in costumes as saints, angels, and devils. Together, the three celebrations, the eve of All Saints', All Saints', and All Souls', were called Hallowmas.

Samhain, with its emphasis on the supernatural, was decidedly pagan. so the Christian missionaries identified their holy days with those observed by the Celts and branded the earlier religion's supernatural deities as evil, and associated them with the devil. Druids were considered evil worshippers of devilish or demonic gods and spirits. The Celtic underworld inevitably became identified with the Christian Hell.

The effects of this act was to diminish but not totally eradicate the beliefs in the traditional gods. Celtic belief in supernatural creatures persisted, while the church made deliberate attempts to define them as being not merely dangerous, but malicious. Followers of the old religion went into hiding and were branded as witches.

Now let's look at the present day celebration of Halloween. There are witches, broomsticks, bats, owls, ghosts, skeletons, death, and monsters. You dress up your children as demons and witches and ghouls and monsters and werewolves and send them out into the street in the darkness to re-enact the Druids' practice of demanding food from people under threat of tricks or curses if they don't comply. Sounds crude but this is just the work of Christianity, and the wide spread domination of all pagan faith. apple bobbing through reasarch that i have made suggest it came from the Christian festival Feralia. Pomona is the Roman goddess of fruit and trees. Her symbol is the apple. Pomona was also a fertility goddess. The Celts believed in the pentagram as an important fertility symbol. As the seeds in the apple form a pentagram shape when cut in half, it was believed that during the mystical Halloween season, the apple could predict future marriages.

Snap Apple Night as referred to form some parts of Ireland is synonymous with "Halloween."

During the annual apple-bobbing festivities, young people would try and bite into apples either floating on water or hanging from a string. It was thought that the first person to bite into an apple would be the next to marry. If it was not for traditions like these, most of these people would never have the opportunity to meet. In this aspect, bobbing for apples was more than a simplistic tradition as it was one that carried the power to alter the lives and futures of entire families and subsequent generations.

Written by Philip Williams

Red ridge research

www.redridge-esp.t83.net

THE COCK LANE POLTERGEIST

In 1762 Cock Lane, a quiet street in the north-west region of the City of London became the epicentre of public hysteria, when alleged poltergeist activity terrorised one of the humble dwellings there. It is hard to imagine a more prolific case of poltergeist activity, with such outreaching effects than what took place over a period of several months at this and nearby locations.

The Cock Lane Poltergeist case as etched itself permanently in the annals of paranormal research for least for the controversy it caused at the time and since, but for the impact it had on both the Methodist and Anglican Churches, the esteemed law courts of London and its most influential dignitaries, but it was also responsible for many heated debates with high-ranking politicians, physicians and respected academics. Charles Dickens is one of several well-known Victorian authors who frequently alluded to the bizarre occurrences at Cock Lane in some of his literary works , and the pictorial satirist William Hogarth referenced the alleged poltergeist in two of his prints.

To appreciate the uniqueness and unprecedented impact of this case we must begin this case study several years earlier and in a previous location. In 1756-57, a money lender in Norfolk, by the name of William Kent, married Elizabeth Lynes, the eldest daughter of a grocer in Lyneham. They eventually moved to nearby Stoke Ferry where Kent ran an inn, and a short time later the local post office.
Their time at Stoke Ferry was to be short-lived and ill-fated. Sadly, during this time Elizabeth died during childbirth. Throughout her pregnancy Elizabeth had been stricken by several illnesses and complications and as a result her younger sister Frances – more fondly known as Fanny had moved in with the couple. Fanny served and devotedly cared for her sister and brother-in-law. So devoted was she that she stayed on after the ill-fated birth and cared for the infant and father.

In time William and Fanny became involved in a relationship. The canon law of that time ruled out any chance of marriage, stating that a widower could not marry the sister of his late wife. This however did not prevent William from travelling to London to seek advice on this matter and was told that as Elizabeth had borne him a living son, a union with Fanny was impossible.

In January 1759, in response to the legal advice he had received, William Kent left Fanny and moved to London, with the intention of 'purchasing a place in some public office'. He hoped that by involving himself in new surroundings and furthering his business prospects he would eventually be able to forget his passion for Fanny.

Fanny's family were strongly opposed to her relationship with Kent and were very vocal in making their views known. Despite this family opposition, Fanny repeatedly sent passionate letters to Kent, pleading with him to take her back into his life. Eventually he succumbed to wishes and allowed her to join him at his lodgings in East Greenwich near London, whereupon the couple lived together in all appearances as man and wife. Again, as with their previous accommodation Fanny and William didn't stay long before moving to lodgings near the Mansion House, but thanks to Fanny's family persistence to spread the news of her illegal relationship, the landlord found out and in an expression of his contempt refused to repay a sum of money Kent loaned him. The sum in question is believed to have been in the region of £20. Kent responded by having him arrested.

As regular church goers at the church of St Sepulchre-without Newgate the couple soon met Richard Parsons, the officiating clerk. To many he was seen as a respectable man. However, in reality Parsons was a drunk and was struggling to provide for his family. William and Fanny confided in Parsons who at first was sympathetic to their situation, and as a result he offered them the use of lodgings in his home at, 20 Cock Lane, located to the north of St Sepulchre's church. The dwelling on Cock lane comprised of a three storey house in a respectable but declining area of London, and had a single room on each floor, connected by a single spiral staircase. While in residence at this address William and Fanny adopted the title of Mr and Mrs Kent. For a while things seemed to working out to their satisfaction and William loaned Parson's the sum of 12 guineas, with the understanding that it repaid at a rate of one guinea per month.

Sometime later, Kent was away attending the wedding of a friend in the country; it was at this time that the first strange noises were reported at the Cock Lane address. Part of the house, (although separate from the apartment used by the 'Kent's') was also occupied by Richard Parsons, his wife and their eleven-year-old daughter, Elizabeth.

William Kent had asked Elizabeth to stay with Fanny during his absence, to help look after her, as at this time Fanny was several months pregnant. Because of the restrictive layout of the house, which included a definite lack of adequate sleeping space, Fanny and Elizabeth were forced to share the same bed. It was during a sleepless night that the two witnessed strange scratching sounds. Mrs. Parsons explained that the noises were probably a result of neighbouring cobbler working late in his shop. However, when the same noises re-occurred some days later, Fanny asked if the cobbler was again working late. On this occasion she was told, he was not.

Another witness to strange phenomena at Cock Lane was James Franzen, the landlord of the nearby Wheat Sheaf public house. While visiting the house one night, Frazen claims to have seen a ghostly white figure ascending the stairs; he was so frightened by the experience he immediately left in terror and made hast back to his home. This same phenomena was also allegedly witnessed on a separate occasion by Parsons while he visited Fanny and his daughter one night.

Because Fanny was only weeks away from giving birth and William was still plagued by painful memories of his late wife's tragic pregnancy, he made arrangements to move to a property at Bartlet's Court in Clerkenwell.

Although all the arrangements had been agreed and finalised the couple were unable to move immediately as renovation being carried out on the new address had not yet been completed. It must also be said that this move was only intended to be a temporary solution.

In January 1760, Fanny fell ill. After the visiting physician diagnosed the early stages of an eruptive fever, it was quickly agreed that their current living accommodation at Cock lane was clearly inadequate for someone in such a critical stage of pregnancy, and Fanny was hastily transported by coach to Bartlet's Court.

The following day, has a result of a sudden deterioration in Fanny's condition, the physician visited again and this time diagnosed that Fanny was experiencing all the symptoms of smallpox, a disease at that time was almost certainly fatal. Obviously distressed by this tragic diagnosis, Fanny responded immediately by sending for an attorney to assure her that the provisions she had made for William were in good order and he would be the main beneficiary of her estates following her death.

On 2 February, 1760, Fanny succumbed to effects of smallpox and died.

As sole executor to Fanny's will he was charged with the responsibility of ordering her coffin. Because of the complex nature of their relationship, this task proved to be somewhat complicated, Kent could not allow a name plate to be attached to the coffin, however, on registering the burial he was unable to withhold a name and had no alternative but to give a name and reluctantly gave her his name.

Inevitably, Fanny's family was notified of her death, whereupon, her sister Ann Lynes, who lived at nearby Pall Mall, attended the funeral held at St John's Church. Eventually Ann learned of the terms of Fanny's will, which left her brothers and sisters half a crown each and the remainder to William Kent. Understandably upset by this, Ann tried to contest the will and was unsuccessful in her efforts to have it blocked in Doctor's Commons. The bulk of Kent's inheritance was Fanny's £150 share of her dead brother Thomas's estate. This also included some land owned by Thomas, sold by the executor of his estate, John Lynes, and Kent received Fanny's share of that too (almost £95). Her family strongly objected to this. As a result of legal problems with Lyne's sale each of Thomas's beneficiaries had to pay £45 in compensation to the purchaser, but Kent refused, claiming that he had already spent the money in settling Fanny's debts. Lynes responded to Kent's refusal by beginning legal proceedings in October 1761 in the Court of Chancery. During the intervening period Kent became a stockbroker, and in 1761 married again.

THE HAUNTING BEGINS

In January 1762, the mysterious noises began again. William Kent had left Cock Lane by this point and another tenant, a Miss Catherine Friend had moved in for a short time, although her stay was short. She moved out when the noises became so frequent and frightening.

It soon became apparent that the noises were emanating predominantly from Elizabeth Parson's bedroom room, and more often than not when she was in attendance there. It may be worth noting also that young Elizabeth was prone to suffering from fits.

According to many witnesses, the strange sounds were very similar to those made by a cat scratching at a wooden chair. In an attempt to discover their source Richard Parsons arranged for a local carpenter to remove the wainscoting from around Elizabeth's bed. Following the failure of this extreme measure to produce any evidence or resolution to the situation, Parsons, in desperation contacted John Moore, the assistant preacher at St Sepulchre's Church.

John Moore was quick to point out that the presence of one ghost had already been recorded at the time when Fanny lay dying. The ghost's identity had been presumed to be that of Fanny's sister Elizabeth. Moore and Parsons therefore decided that the current ghost must surely be that of Fanny Lynes herself.

In the anxious days and weeks that followed, Moore and Parsons devised a clever method of communication with the alleged ghost. By using a system of knocks; one knock for 'yes' and two knocks for 'no' as a result of this system and its subsequent responses the two men came to the conclusion that Fanny Lynes had apparently been murdered by William Kent. Even though many people associated with this case were in agreement with Moore and parsons' conclusion, not surprisingly, no charge was ever made against Kent.

Although Moore's attempts may be regarded as primitive at best, and most certainly unreliable by modern day investigative methods, the suggestion seemed to be that Fanny Lynes had not died from the effects of smallpox but rather from arsenic poisoning. The deadly poisoning had allegedly been administered by Kent two hours before Fanny's death. The understandable conclusion, based on this bizarre method of gaining information was that the ghost responsible for producing the noises was indeed, Fanny Lynes, and was searching for justice.

In the 18th century it was a quite common belief that restless spirits would return from the dead in search of justice against the persons responsible for their deaths; despite the fact that no legal action could be instigated as a result of the bizarre nature of the evidence, the matter was taken very seriously by influential people in London's academic society.

Ann Lynes complained at the time of her sister's funeral that the coffin lid had been screwed down and she was therefore unable to see her sister's corpse. Moore, deduced from this that if Fanny had been poisoned, there would be no visible scars as a result of smallpox, a fact that Kent would have understandably have tried to hide.

As a practising Methodist priest, Moore was inclined to believe the ghost, however, for added support he enlisted the aid of his colleague Reverend Thomas Broughton. On the 5 January Broughton visited Cock Lane, and subsequently agreed that the ghost was indeed real. The story spread throughout London and *'The Public Ledger'*, a popular newspaper of the time began to publish detailed accounts of the events. Has a result of the publicity from this, Kent fell under public suspicion as a murderer.

SEANCES

Once Kent became aware of the allegations made against him in *The Public Ledger* and the interest it had generated, he was determined to clear his name, and accompanied by a witness went to see John Moore.

Upon meeting Moore showed him the list of questions that he and Parsons intended to ask the ghost. One of the first questions regarded Fanny and Kent's marital status, whereupon he reluctantly admitted to the preacher that he and Fanny had never married.

Moore was at pains to tell Kent that he didn't believe him to be a murderer, and suggested that the spirit's presence indicated that there was some kind of dark message to be passed on, and urged him to go to Parsons' house, where he might be convinced of the ghosts reality.

On 12 January, Kent succumbed to Moores wishes, he visited Cock Lane accompanied by two physicians who had attended Fanny in her last days, also in attendance was Reverend Broughton.

All those in attendance gathered on the upper floor in Elizabeth Parsons' bedroom. The young girl was prepared for bed. The audience sat around the bed which had been placed in the centre of the room. A warning was issued, stating that the ghost was sensitive disbelief, and all who were present should afford it the utmost respect.

Mary Frazer, a relative of Parsons began the séance. She ran round the room shouting "Fanny, Fanny, why don't you come? Do come, pray Fanny!" Nothing happened, and Moore offered the embarrassed explanation that the spirit would not show because the sitters were making too much noise. He then asked everyone to leave the room and would attempt to contact the ghost by stamping his foot. Ten minutes later everyone was informed that the ghost had returned and that they should all, quietly re-enter the room. When everyone was settled and silence prevailed Moore began to ask the questions he had listed with Parsons:

"Are you the wife of Mr. Kent? – Two knocks (no)

"Did you die naturally?" – Two knocks.

"By poison?" – One knock (yes)

When Moore had asked a few more questions a member of the audience interrupted with a question of his own: "Kent, ask this ghost if you shall be hanged!" Moore complied the man's request on Kent's behalf and was answered by a single knock. Kent was furious at this response and exclaimed: "Thou art a lying spirit, thou art not the ghost of my Fanny. She would never have said such a thing!"

Has time passed it became apparent that the ghost appeared to follow Elizabeth Parsons. On 14 January she was moved to the house of Mr Bray and in the presence of two respected academics the knocking sounds were heard again.

On 18 January, another séance was held at Cock Lane, this time, those present included, Kent, the apothecary and local parish priest and incumbent of St John, Clerkenwell, Reverend Stephen Aldrich. On this occasion a priest who used a candle to look under the bed, the ghost 'refused' to answer. Frazer, the self-appointed medium explained that the ghost would not answer because she did not like the light. Silence ensued for several minutes, after which Moore asked if the ghost would appear in court against Kent, Frazer, however, refused to ask this question.

While Fanny and William Kent had lived at Cock Lane they had employed a maid, Esther 'Carrots' Carlisle, so named because of her red hair. Carrots had by this time moved on to another employer and knew nothing about the haunting, however, her evidence of event during the time of Fanny's alleged poisoning was considered crucial. When asked about the fatal event Carrot's informed Moore that Fanny had been unable to speak in the days leading up to her death. She was also at pains to emphasise that Fanny and William lived quite happily together and were a very loving couple. Kent arrived later in the proceedings, this time accompanied by James Franzen, (the landlord of the Wheat Sheaf public house), and the reverends William Dodd and Thomas Broughton.

Although Frazer began the séance in her usual bizarre manner, Moore sent her out, apparently irritated by her noisy behaviour. There were another twenty or so other people present who Moore asked to leave the room, before calling them back in some minutes later. The séance that followed was this time centred around Carrots Carlisle, who questioned the ghost directly.

"Are you my mistress?" – One knock (yes), followed by scratching
"Are you angry with me Madam?" – One knock
"Then I am sure Madam, you may be ashamed of yourself for I have hurt you in my life."

When the séance eventually ended only Frazer and Franzen remained in the room. Franzen was said to be so afraid that he could not move, whereupon Frazer asked him if he would like to pray. Franzen was angered apparently when he discovered he was incapable of prayer. The séance resumed a short time later but Franzen elected to return to his home at this point. The landlord's plight did not end there, however, when he and his wife retired to bed for the night it is reported that the two were disturbed all night by mysterious knocking sounds in their bedchamber.

INVESTIGATION

On 20 January another séance was held, this time at the home of Mr. Bruin on nearby Hosier Lane. One of the people present at this event was bent on exposing the whole affair as a hoax, and later sent his account of the nights proceedings to *The London Chronicle*. During the séance a member of the group who obviously disagreed with the ghost existence positioned himself near to Elizabeth's bed. When the ghost sympathisers asked him to move he refused, at which point, most of the party left. The gentleman in question asked Parsons' if he would allow the removal of Elizabeth to another room at his own house, Parsons refused.

When later questioned about the séance Elizabeth admitted she had seen the ghost and was not frightened by it. At 7am on the morning after the séance the knocking and scratching noises resumed. Following the usual questions about the cause of Fanny's death and who was responsible, the interrogation turned to her body, which lay in the vaults of St John's Church.

On 22 January Parsons' agreed to move his daughter to the house of Reverend Aldrich for further testing. When Reverend Penn arrived at Aldrich's house, Parsons told him that Elizabeth was not there and refused to reveal her whereabouts. Parsons had spoken to friends and was apparently worried that Kent had been busy with his own investigations. On the same night Parsons moved his daughter to St Bartholomews Hospital where another séance was carried out. The night remain eventless until 6 a.m. at which time three scratching noises were heard, apparently while Elizabeth lay sleeping. There were approximately twenty people in attendance, most of which declared that the affair was a deception. When Elizabeth awoke, she began to cry. Every effort was made to comfort her, and to assure her that she was safe. As Elizabeth eventually recomposed herself she admitted that her fears were for her father, who would surely be ruined if he were suspected of imposture. She subsequently added to her admission that although she appeared to be asleep, she had in fact been fully awake and aware of the conversation around her.

Although at first the bizarre events at Cock Lane were of little interest to the general public, it didn't take long once reports began to appear in some of London's prestigious newspaper for interest to accumulate to an almost hysterical level. The story spread across London and by the middle of January the crowds were gathering outside the property in Cock Lane, to such an extent that passage through the formed quiet, narrow lane, was impassable.

Being a man of sound business sense, Parsons recognised the potential of the affair to provide him a tidy income, and thus began to charge visitors an entrance fee to 'talk' with the ghost.

Samuel Fludyer, Lord mayor of London was approached on 23 January by Alderman Gosling, John Moore and Parsons, who informed him of their experiences. Fludyer had recently had an embarrassing experience with a similar case involving a fraudster by the name of Elizabeth Canning, and still stinging from the ordeal refused to have Kent and Parsons arrested for murder and conspiracy respectively. Instead, because of the common interest by the public at large and fearful of upsetting the masses, he ordered that Elizabeth Parsons be tested at Reverend Aldrich's house.

Elizabeth was the subject of study two further séances held on 23-24 January. Despite accepting the Lord Mayor's decision, Parson asked for, "some persons connected with the girl to be present, to divert her in the day-time." This request was refused, as were two other's of a similar nature. Aldrich and Penn insisted that the event should only be attended by "persons of strict character and reputation."

The refusal of his request clearly annoyed Parsons, who defended his actions in an article in the *Public Ledge*. This prompted Aldrich and Penn to issue a pointed retort in *Lloyd's Evening Post*.

On 26 January, Elizabeth was taken to the house of Jane Armstrong, where she slept in a hammock. Despite the choice of sleeping arrangements the noises continued which only strengthened the resolve of the ghost's supporters. The press carried on reporting the case with great vigour and has a result members of high society began to take interest in the bizarre events of Elizabeth Parson and Cock Lane.

On 30 January, Horace Warpole, 4th Earl of Orford, the Duke of York, Lady Northumberland, Lady Mary Coke and Lord Herford visited Cock Lane. After struggling through the crowds the noble visitors were ultimately disappointed; the *Public Advertiser* observed that 'the noise is now generally deferred till seven in the morning, it being necessary to vary the time, that the imposition may be the better carried on."

EXPOSURE

At the end of January, 1762 a committee of people to be involved in the investigation of Elizabeth Parsons and Cock Lane had been formed by Lord Dartmouth and Aldrich. This committee included, the matron of a local lying-in hospital, her role was to be principal lady-in-waiting, the critic and controversionalist Bishop John Douglas, Dr George Macaulay and Captain Wilkinson, a man who famously attended a previous séance armed with a pistol and stick; the pistol to shoot the source of the knocking and the stick to help him make a hasty escape. Ironically, the ghost did not appear on that occasion, also on the committee were James Penn and John Moore. However, the most prominent and influential member of the committee was Dr Samuel Johnson, who subsequently documented the séance, which was held on 1 February 1762:

"On the night of the 1st of February many gentlemen eminent for their rank and character were, by the invitation of the reverend Mr. Aldrich, of Clerkenwell, assembled at his house, for the examination of the noises supposed to be made by a departed spirit, for the detection of some enormous crime. About ten at night the gentlemen met in the chamber in which the girl, supposed to be disturbed by a spirit, had, with proper caution, been put to bed by several ladies. They sat rather more than an hour, and on hearing nothing, went down stairs, when they interrogated the father of the girl, who denied, in the strongest terms, any knowledge or belief of fraud. The supposed spirit had before publicly promised, by an affirmative knock, that it would attend one of the gentlemen into the vault under the Church of St John, Clerkenwell, where the body is deposited, and give a token of her presence there, by a knock upon her coffin; it was therefore determined to make this trial of the existence or veracity of the supposed spirit. While they were enquiring and deliberating, they were summoned into the girl's bedchamber by some ladies who were near her bed, and who had heard knocks and scratches. When the gentlemen entered, the girl declared that she felt the spirit like a mouse upon her back, and was required to hold her hands out of bed. From that time, though the spirit was very solemnly required to manifest its existence by appearance, by impression on the hand or body of any present, by scratches, knocks, or any other agency, no evidence of any preter-natural power was exhibited. The spirit was then very seriously advertised that the person to whom the promise was made of striking the coffin, was then about to visit the vault, and that the performance of the promise was then claimed. The company at one o'clock went into the church, and the gentleman to whom the promise was made, went with another into the vault. The spirit was solemnly required to perform its promise, but nothing more than silence ensued: the person supposed to be accused by the spirit, then went down with several others, but no effect was perceived. Upon the return they examined the girl, but could draw no confession from her. Between two and three she desired and was permitted to go home with her father. It is therefore, the opinion of the whole assembly, that the child has some art of making or counterfeiting a particular noise, and that there is no agency of any higher cause.

- Samuel Johnson (1762)

As a direct result of the failure of this séance, Moore told Kent he believed it was an imposter, and he would do everything in his power to reveal it. Kent was cheered by this statement and asked him to admit the truth and write an avadavat to that effect, so as to end the affair and clear his name and reputation. Moore refused, claiming that he still believed that the spirit's presence was a reminder of his sin. This was a view held by many, including Elizabeth Parsons mother, who believed that the alleged ghost of Elizabeth Kent had disapproved of her sister's new relationship.

On 3 February, However, another séance was held, at which the knocking continued. Parsons was in an unenviable situation by this time, and was keen to prove the ghost was not an impostor. He therefore allowed his daughter to be examined again, this time at a house on The Strand. These séances lasted from 7 to 10 February, a further séance was also held at a house in Covent Garden from 14 February.

At the latter séance, Elizabeth Parsons was subjected to various bizarre tests, including being swung from an hammock, her hands and feet being extended beyond its sides, so they remain in full view of the audience gathered around her. The noises commenced but stopped when Elizabeth was forced to place her hands outside the bed. On the following two nights there were no taps or scratching to be heard. This period of silence did little to alleviate the suspicion held by the critics and Elizabeth was informed that if no more sounds were heard by Sunday 21 February, she and her father would be committed to Newgate prison.

On a subsequent séance, Elizabeth's maids saw her conceal a small piece of wood about her person, they obviously informed the investigators of this infringement of the strict rules of conduct. No one was surprised when scratching sounds were heard but the observers concluded that Elizabeth was responsible and that her father had forced her to produce them. Elizabeth was allowed home not long after this discovery.

On 25 February, a pamphlet was published called *The Mystery Revealed,* which is believed to have been written by Oliver Goldsmith. At this time Kent was still trying desperately to clear his name and went to the vault of St John's Church, accompanied by Reverend Aldrich, the undertaker, the clerk and the parish sexton. The reason for this groups visit was to prove beyond any doubt that a recent newspaper report, which claimed that the body of Fanny Kent had been removed from its coffin and was thus the reason why the spirit had failed to knock. When the undertaker removed the coffin lid all those present were rendered speechless by shock and horror. Moore was so shocked and subsequently affected by the sight that he made all haste to publish his retraction:

"In justice to the person, whose reputation has been attacked in a most gross manner, by the pretended Ghost in Cock Lane; to check the credulity of the weak; to defeat the attempts of the malicious, and to prevent further impostion, on account of this absurd phenomenon, I do hereby certify, that though, from the several attendances on this occasion, I have not been able to point out, how, and in what manner, those knockings and scratching, of the supposed ghost, were *contrived, performed,* and *continued;* yet those knockings and scratching were the effects of some artful, wicked contrivance; and that I was, in a more especial manner, convinced of it being such, on the first of this month, when I attended with several persons of rank and character, who assembled at the Reverend Mr. Aldrich's, Clerkenwell, in order to examine into this iniquitous imposition upon the Public. Since which time, I have not seen the child, nor heard the noises; and think myself in duty bound to add, that the injured person (when present to hear himself accused by the pretended ghost) has not, by his behavior, given the least ground of suspicion, but has preserved that becoming steadfastness, which nothing, I am persuaded, but innocence could inspire.

- John Moore (1762)

Has sincere as this retraction appeared to be, it was not enough to prevent him from subsequently being charged by the authorities of conspiracy, along with Richard Parsons and his wife, Mary Frazer and Richard James, a local tradesman.

THE CASE IN COURT

The trial was held at the Guild Hall on July 10, 1762. The presiding judge was Lord Chief Justice William Murray. All five defendants were in attendance when the proceedings began at 10 a.m. The charges brought by William Kent against all five defendants for a conspiracy designed and perpetrated by the defendants to take away his life by charging him with the murder of Frances Lynes by giving her poison whereof she died."

The courtroom was packed with spectators, who witnessed William Kent reveal his controversial former relationship with Frances Lynes, and his account of her resurrection as "Scratching Fanny", (so named because of the scratching noises made by the alleged ghost).

James Franzen took the stand and his story was corroborated Esther "Carrors Carlisle". Dr. Cooper, had administered medicines to Fanny as she lay dying told how he always suspected the noises in Cock Lane were a trick, later that same day James Jones, the apothecary who had attended Fanny with Dr. Cooper supported his statement. Several other witnesses described how the hoax had been revealed.

Richard James was accused by the prosecution's last witness of being responsible for some of the more offensive published material in the *Public Ledger*.

The defense witnesses statement were in stark contrast however. Some of these persons had cared for Elizabeth Parson, and still believed that the ghost was real. Other witnesses who testified that the ghost was genuine were the carpenter who had been instructed to remove the wainscoting from Elizabeth's bedchamber, and Catherine Friend, a subsequent tenant of the Cock Lane house for a short while before leaving in fear of the noises, after the 'Kent's' had vacated the premises.

Reverend Thomas Broughton and Reverend Ross were also called, the latter was one of the gentlemen who had questioned the ghost; Chief Justice Murray asked him whether he had puzzled the ghost or had he in fact been puzzled by the ghost. John Moore was supported by many of his esteemed associates, the Arch Bishop of Canterbury, Thomas Secker being one. A letter was presented to the judge from the Arch Bishop, Chief Justice Murray merely placed it in his pocket, unopened and declared that it had no possible relevance to the case in hand. Richard James and Richard Parsons also received support from several witnesses, some of whom testified that despite knowing of Parsons drinking problem could not believe him to be guilty.

The trial ended the same day, at around 9.30 p.m., after which the judge spent ninety minutes summing up, however, the jury took only fifteen minutes to reach a verdict of guilty for all five defendants. On the following Monday two further individuals were found guilty of defaming William Kent and were each fined £50.

On 22 November the conspirators were brought back to court but sentencing was delayed in the hope that those involved could agree the level of payable to Kent. Has this agreement was not forthcoming court was re-intervened on 27 January 1763 and they were all committed to the King's Bench Prison until 11 February. By this time John Moore and Richard James had agreed to pay Kent £588; after which they were both pardoned and released by order of Justice Wilmot. However, the following day the rest were sentenced:

"The court chusing that Mr. Kent, who had been so much injured on the occasion, should receive some reparation by punishment of the offenders, deferred giving judgment for seven or eight months, *in hopes that the parties might make it up in the meantime.* Accordingly, the clergyman, and tradesman agreed to pay Mr. Kent a round sum – some say between £500 and £600 to purchase their pardon, and were, therefore, dismissed with a severe reprimand. The father was ordered to be set in the pillory three times in one month – once at the end of Cock Lane; Elizabeth his wife to be imprisoned one year; and Mary Frazer six months in Bridewell, with hard labour. The father appearing to be out of his mind at the time he was first to stand in the pillory, the execution of that part of his sentence was deferred to another day, when, as well as the other day of his standing there, the populace took so much compassion on him, that instead of using him ill, they made a handsome subscription for him.

-Annual Register, vol. cxlii. And Gentleman's Magazine, 1762

FAR-REACHING CONSEQUENCES

The Cock Lane poltergeist case had many and varied far-reaching consequences, not least the religious controversy it caused between the Methodist and orthodox Anglican Churches. The belief of a spiritual afterlife is common-place in most religions and the alleged manifestation of a spirit in the 'real world' is taken by many to be confirmation of that belief. John Wesley, one of the founders of Methodism, (mentioned in the earlier chapter, (The Epworth Rectory Poltergeist), was himself heavily influenced of a supposed haunting in his home.

In its early days Methodism was the target of much criticism for its position on witchcraft and magic. Although far from a united religion, Methodism was almost synonymous with a belief in the supernatural. It is no surprise, therefore, that many of its followers were convinced that the ghost of Cock Lane, was indeed real, contrary to those in the Anglican community, who considered such things to be a relic of the country's Catholic past.

This unfortunate situation could not have been displayed any clearer than it was between the Methodist John Moore and the Anglican Stephen Aldrich. In 1845, Horace Warpole referred to this case in his memoirs. Warpole had been present at one of the séances and subsequently accused the Methodist clergymen of actively colluding to establish the existence of the ghost. He described how the Methodist clergymen had made a point of being close to Elizabeth Parsons during the proceedings and implied that the church would recompense her father for his troubles.

Samuel Johnson, however, was committed to his Christian faith and shared the views of author Joseph Glanvill, who in his 1681 work *Saducismus Triumphatus,* wrote entensively of his concern over the advances made against religion and a belief in witchcraft, by atheism and skepticism. Johnson was firm in his belief that for an afterlife not to exist was an appalling thought, but, although he thought that spirits could protect and counsel the living, he kept himself distant from the more credulous Methodists, and recognized that his religion required proof of an afterlife. His perspective on the matter can be clearly seen in his discussions with his biographer, James Boswell, who said:

Sir, I make a distinction between what a man may experience by the mere strength of his imagination, and what imagination cannot possibly produce. Thus, suppose I should think I saw a form, and heard a voice cry, "Johnson, you are a very wicked fellow, and unless you repent you will certainly be punished;" my own unworthiness is so deeply impressed upon my mind, that I might imagine I thus saw and hear, and therefore I should not believe that an external communication had been made to me. But if a form should appear, and a voice tell me that a particular man had died at a particular place, and a particular hour, a fact which I had no apprehension of, nor any means of knowing, and this fact, with all its circumstances, should afterwards be unquestionably proved, I should, in that case, be persuaded that I had supernatural intelligence imparted to me.

THE WALDEGRAVES
CHASING THE IDENTITY OF THE NUN OF BORLEY RECTORY

The Waldegraves, an influential Roman Catholic family, were intimately connected with Borley for some three hundred years, during which period they were patrons of the church and held the Manor of Borley. A descendant of Sir Richard Waldegrave (who died in 1402) was Sir Edward Waldgrave, the first member of this family actively connected with Borley. He was imprisoned during the reign of Edward V1 for his loyalty to the princess, afterwards Queen Mary, and he received from her the Manor of Chewton, in Somersetshire. Chewton Priory, Bath, is the present seat of the Waldegrave family.

Sir Edward Waldegrave (c. 1517 – 61) was Member of Parliament for Essex and Chancellor of the Duchy of Lancaster. He was knighted at the Coronation of Queen Mary in 1553. After Mary's death he suffered a reverse of fortune, and he was a prisoner in the Tower of London (his crime was permitting the saying of a Mass at Borley), where he died on September 1, 1561. He married Frances (who died in 1599), daughter of Sir Edward Neville, and had three sons and three daughters. His wife survived him for thirty-years, taking for her second husband Chedick Paulet, third son of William Paulet, first Marquis of Winchester. He was Governor of Southampton. The Paulet arms can be seen on the Waldegrave tomb. Sir Edward Waldegrave, his wife, and their six children are depicted on the very ornate tomb at the north-east corner of the nave in Borley Church. I will describe in some detail:

This alter-tomb, fourteen feet high, is made of clunch (i.e., indurate clay or hard chalk), with painted recumbent effigies of Sir Edward and Frances. The man is in plate armour and ruff, the woman in flat cap and large ruff, with crests at the feet of both effigies. The tomb has panelled sides, with the kneeling figures of their three sons and three daughters, each with an inscription and coat of arms. The canopy of the tomb has a coffered soffit, resting on six Corinthian columns. The cornice is surmounted by cresting and achievement of arms, and a shield of arms. At angles, there are figures of cherubs holding cartouches of arms. The monument has a marginal inscription in Latin and a record of other alliances of the family. It is an outstanding example of sixteenth-century work and appears to be in perfect condition.

On the north wall of the chancel is a painted tablet of Magdala Waldegrave (third daughter of Sir Edward), wife of John Southcote, which was put up to her memory after her death in 1598. She is shown kneeling in prayer, wearing a flat headdress and ruff, with tight fitting bodice and loose skirt, and a sleeveless mantle over her shoulders. The monument is flanked by Ionic columns, with a shield of arms above cornice.

The Rev. Frances G.S. Nicolle, Vicar of St Thomas's, Bethnal Green, in a letter to me dated October 18, 1942, says:

I have come across a piece of information which may be of sufficient interest to pass on to you. It would seem that Sir Edward Waldegrave was not, after all, the first of that family to be associated with Borley, but his grandfather, also named Edward. This how the story works out: Sir Thomas (great-grandson of Sir Richard, the Speaker of the House of Commons) married Elizabeth, eldest daughter of Sir John Fray, and died in 1500. He was succeeded by William, the eldest of his three sons. The second son, Edward (ancestor of the present family), had settled at Borley, in Essex, and married Elizabeth, daughter of John Chayney, of Devon. He too died in 1500, and was succeeded by his only son, John Waldegrave, who married Lora, daughter of Sir John Rochester, who died in 1514. Sir Edward, who married Frances, daughter of Sir Edward Neville, and died in the Tower under Elizabeth in 1561, was the eldest son of this marriage.

It is highly probable that the bodies of the Waldegraves, depicted on the tomb, were interred at Borley. There is a crypt under Borley Church, and our efforts to find it will be described later. As I recorded in my previous monograph on the Borley case, Miss Ethel Bull informed us that, many years previously, coffins in the crypt had been paranormally moved – as in the classic case of the 'haunted vault' at Christ Church, Barbados. It is presumed that the coffins were those of the Waldegrave family. From time to time phenomena in Borley Church have been recorded.

Sir Edward's second son, Nicholas, inherited the Borley property. Mrs Georgina Dawson says:

Nicholas Waldegrave, the second son, sometimes called Sir Nicholas, but I am not sure this is correct. He inherited Borley, and from him all the later Borley Waldegraves are descended. Nicholas must have been born between 1550 and 1561, when his father died, and he himself died on June 19, 1621, possessed of the Manor of Borley Hall, ten acres (probably woodland) in Bulmer, and some unspecified share in the church and Manor of Langenhoo ....
Nicholas's eldest son, Philip Waldegrave, married twice .... His eldest son John by the first wife appears to have had only the one son, Philip, who is listed as a recusant in 1715, and whose death the Borley Waldegrave came to an end, and the estates passed to Jmaes, Lord Waldegrave.
He is later made an Earl. Philip Waldegrave died in 1720-21.
The Waldegraves lived at Borley Hall, on the river Stour, built in the first half of the sixteenth century. It is marked on modern Ordnance Survey maps, and has long been occupied by the Payne family.
Borley Manor house (now called Borley Place) is the old house nearly opposite the Rectory, and is the residence of Mr Basil Payne. In the cellars are considerable remains of a much earlier building, and associated with it is the familiar story of a 'secret tunnel'.
Ancient maps of the district show only two houses at Borley – the 'Hall' and the 'Place'.
As for Borley Rectory, it is certain that earlier buildings have been erected on the site. The Herringham family had a rectory there, and there are memorials to them in Borley Church. In my previous monograph I assumed that the Waldegraves also had a house where the rectory now stands – or rather, stood. I was wrong. But it is possible – even likely – that the Waldegraves had a chaplain's house on the site. It is certain that there *was* a rectory at Borley in the sixteenth century, with a high degree of probability that it was built opposite the church, where our 'haunted house' stood. During our investigations we discovered foundations of an ancient building in the cellars of the Rectory. It had been constructed of the old two-inch bricks.
Concerning the 'monastery' tradition, it is very unlikely that such a foundation ever existed at Borley. But just across the river Stour, that here forms the boundary between Essex and Suffolk, there *was* a Priory. Mrs Dawson says:

But though there was no monastery, etc., actually on the site of the present Rectory, there was a Priory near Borley, whose lands probably adjoined Borley, and as the Priory was Benedictine, and the land at Borley owned by the Benedictines, this must be the explanation of the tradition of 'Borley Monastery'. But so far as can be discovered, the only link between the Bendedictine Priory and Borley was that the Benedictine Order had 'Free Warren' at Borley, and the later connexion of the Waldegraves with the Benedictines would further confuse the matter.

The ruins of the Priory are still extant.

We need not have concerned ourselves with the Waldegraves at all, except for two reasons: (a) the fact that the name 'Waldegrave' was recurrent in the Planchette scripts, with the implication – even the assertion – that a member of this family (whose name was later given as 'Henry') strangled 'Mary Lairre,' the nun-ghsot, in 1667; and (b) for the theory evolved by Mrs georgina Dawson, of Leathenhead, near Colchester, that the nun-ghost was Arabella Waldegrave.

As for 'Henry Waldergrave', we know two members of the family whose Christian name was 'Henry', and neither could have been concerned with 'Mary Lairre,' if she died in 1667. One 'Henry' is rthe first Lord Waldergrave, created a peer by James 11. Of course he was a Roman Catholic, and he died in exile in 1689, when a member of King James'ss uite. He was born in 1660, and was created Baron Waldergrave of Chewton in 1686. He married Henrietta Fitzjames (1670 – 1730), the natural daughter of James 11 and Arabella Churchill. Their sons were James, first Earl Waldergrave (1684 – 1741), and Henry Waldegrave (our second 'Henry'), who died a bachelor in 1792. Their daughter was Arabella Waldegrave, of whom more anon. Mr Winston Churchill is a collataeral descendant of this family.

So it is apparent that in 1667 our first Henry was only seven years old, and his son, Hnery, was not even born. But the records of the Waldegrave family are both confused and confusing, and there have been other 'Henry's' who flourished at about the time that 'Mary Lairre'did. If there were I have not come across them. Anyway, it would be unwise to depend on the Planchette scripts for the name of 'Mary's' strangler.

ARABELLA WALDEGRAVE

On April 23, 1943, I had a letter from Mrs dawson (who was a stranger to me), asking for particulars of the clothing of the 'nun' alleged to haunt Borley Rectory. She told me that she had been doing some research work into the history of Borley, 'and what caused such powerful effects there'. She remarked that 'My inquiries are not yet complete, but I feel I am on the right lines and that the lady [the nun-ghost] was Arabella Waldegrave, born in 1687, daughter of Hnery, first Lord Waldegrave and Henrietta Fitzjames, and a grandchild of King Jmaes 11.'

This remarkable information was of the greatest interest, as it tended to demolish, at one blow, our theory (based on the Planchette records) that the nun might be a French girl named Mary Lairre. Mrs Dawson kindly offered to let me have her notes accumulated during the research work, and these duly arrived on June 12, 1943.

Her typed 'notes' turned out to be a *dossier* of Borley, the church, the many rectors dating from 1313, the Rectory, the 'castle', the 'monastery', and the Waldegraves, running to 20,000 words! She has done a really magnificent piece of research work, and a history of Borley could be compiled from her records. She had no absolute *proof* that Arabella was the Borley nun-ghost – but she *did* prove that, after tracing her early history, the girl vanished into thin air – without trace. This would be remarkable enough in such a distinguished family as the Waldegraves, whose contemporary records are available. But a king's grandchild should so disappear is in the nature of a phenomenon. But that Arabella *did* disappear seems certain.

Briefly, Mrs Dawson's story is this. During the period of the fight for the Protestant succession James 11 and his Court fled to Paris. This was in 1688. The Walegraves, being staunch Catholics, went with them – so did little Arabella, then aged one year. Arabella's early girlhood was spent with the Court at Saint-Germain, and at the age of seven she was sent to the convent school of the Benedictines at Pontoise, near Paris, where aunt and cousin were nuns (some fifteen members of the Waldegrave family professed and became nuns.) Arabella's name is mentioned several times in the convents archives. Apparently, Arabella was a naughty girl, and she left – or was dismissed from – Pontoise. According to Foley's Records, she went to Paris and became a nun. And that is the last we hear of her. Every other member of the Waldegrave family has been accounted for, but not Arabella. It was as if the earth had swallowed her up.

The above are all *facts* I possess about Arabella. But from Mrs Dawson's researches, it has been assumed that the girl eventually became a spy or agent for the Stuart Pretenders, or perhaps for the British Government in London. And there is also a theory that Arabella finally found her way to Borley, where perhaps, she was murdered. Hence the 'nun-ghost.' Mrs Dawson may have further evidence supporting this contention; but if so I have not seen it. I understand that she is publishing the full story of her discoveries. It will be read with the greatest interest.

During her researches Mrs Dawson discovered that Arabella's mother, Henrietta Waldegrave, *did* become a spy for the British Government and was expelled from Paris in 1695. She was sent to a convent, escaped and returned to England to oppose the Stuart Pretenders.

It must have been fairly easy for any member of the Waldegrave family to escape to – or from – the Continent, as in addition to being the Lords of the Manor of Borley, they also owned Langenhoo, a lonely spot on the Essex marshes, not far from Borley, and near the sea. And the Rector of Borley was also Rector of Lagenhoo, an ideal place for the smuggling over of priests – or resusant nuns! Arabella's mother, Henrietta, died in 1730. Her grandmother also died in 1730, aged about eighty.

If our information about Arabella is so scanty we know a little more about her grandmother, and I cannot resist giving Lord Macaulay's remarks concerning her. He says:

1685. Soon after the Restoration, in the gay and dissolute times which have been celebrated by the lively pen of Hamilton, James, young and ardent in the pursuit of pleasure, had been attracted by Arabella Churchill, one of the maids of honour who waited on his first wife. The young lady was plain: but the taste of James was not nice: and she became his avowed mistress. She was the daughter of a poor Cavalier knight who haunted Whitehall, and made himself ridiculous by publishing a dull and affected folio, long forgotten, in praise of monarchy and monarchs. The necessities of the Churchills were pressing: their loyalty was ardent; and their only feeling about Arabella's seduction seems to have been joyful surprise that so homely a girl should have attained such high preferment.

Such is the reward of virtue! Arabella Churchill's brother, John Churchill, became the first Duke of Marlborough.

Well, I am grateful to Mrs Dawson for her records, which Canon Phythian-Adams too has perused with much interest. So now we have two claimants (there are others) to the honour of haunting Borley Rectory: 'Mary Lairre' and Arabella Waldegrave. As I have stated, I have seen no proofs that the latter ever visited Borley, either in the flesh or in the spirit. On the other hand, we have a few clues or 'indicators' – for what they are worth – pointing to Mary Lairre as the nun-ghost, and these I will enumerate later. What Canon Phythian-Adams thinks of the Arabella nun-ghost theory, and his observations, will be found in the next file.

I cannot close this chapter without mentioning that Borley Rectory is not the only alleged haunted house that has been associated with the Waldegrave family. Strawberry Hill, near Teddington, is another. Strawberry Hill was purchased by Horace Warpole in 1748. He converted an old cottage into a castellated pseudo-florid=Gothic monstrosity, very flimsy, little better than lath and plaster (Warpole boasted that he had 'outlived three sets of battlements') and turned it into a sort of museum. He filled it with artistic treasures which were dispersed in 1842. At his death in 1797 he bequeathed the property to the Hon Mrs. Anne Damer, the sculptress, the reversion of the house to pass at her death to the Dowager Countess of Waldegrave. Actually, Mrs. Damer parted with it before she died, and the Waldegraves came into possession. I do not know the details of the alleged haunting. The house has, of course, been much altered since the time of Warpole, who here wrote his romantic *Castle of Otranto* (1764), and the still more famous *Letters*. It was here, too that Warpole established his private 'Strawberry Hill Press' in August 1757.

HALLOWEEN SUPERSTATIONS

This article is about Halloween superstitions. The first one ill kick off with is black cats. Black cats have been symbolised from the dark ages. Today it's on decorations for Halloween. When witch hunts were commonplace. Solitary women mainly the elderly were often accused of witchcraft and their pet cats were said to be their "familiars," or demonic animals that had been given to them by the devil.

Another medieval myth told that Satan turned himself into a cat when socializing with witches. But nowadays, black cats aren't synonymous with bad luck and mischief everywhere — in Ireland, Scotland and England, it's considered good luck for a black cat to cross your path.

Also sailors considered having a ship cat. and they would pacifically want a black cat because they believe it would bring them good luck. Sometimes, fishermen's wives would keep black cats at home too, in the hope that they would be able to use their influence to protect their husbands at sea. the cat in Egyptian mythology was also worshiped.

Another superstition connected to Halloween are bats. Medieval folklore described bats as witches or familiars, and seeing a bat on Halloween was considered to be quite an ominous sign. One myth was that if a bat was spotted flying around one's house three times, it meant that someone in that house would soon die. There is a prominent part of modern folklore about bats. People imagine them as the transformed bodies or souls of dead people who are not at peace and who prowl the night sucking the blood of human victims. Folklore and linking bats to vampires is particularly intriguing because there are, in reality, three species of bats that feed on the blood of birds and mammals. All three are restricted exclusively to New World tropical regions where their main prey are domestic livestock, primarily cattle, and fowl.

Spiders also join the ranks of bats and black cats in folklore as being evil companions of witches during medieval times. One superstition held that if a spider falls into a candle-lit lamp and is consumed by the flame, witches are nearby. And if you spot a spider on Halloween the spirit of a deceased loved one is watching over you.

BLACK-EYED PEOPLE
THEY STEEL YOUR SOUL

Wayne Ridsdel

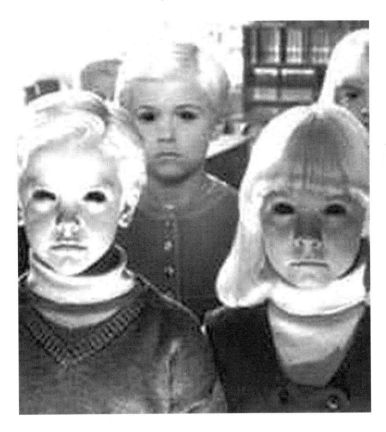

One day you might get a knock on your door or window, and when you open it a child is standing there asking to come in, or maybe asking for a lift. An innocent scenario, you may think, but if recent reports are to be believed you could well be opening the door to your worst ever nightmare. Forget the 'mad axeman,' the 'insane neighbourhood serial killer,' or the 'escaped murderer from the nearby prison,' Once you allow entrance to the Black-eyed kid, or sometimes the black-eyed person (often in the guise of a frail looking lady or gentleman), then your life as a functioning human being is over.

BEKs (Black-Eyed Kids) and BEPs (Black-Eyed People) as are a relatively new terrifying phenomena that until now have been dismissed as mere urban legends. However, there has been a dramatic increase in the number of reports concerning BEP and BEK experiences.

Let's familiarize ourselves with some of the facts, claimed to be true by alleged BEK and BEP experiencers:
Sometimes you feel someone is staring at you, then you become aware of jet black eyes locked onto you. They always want something from you, it may be a ride, or they might want to use your telephone. Their goal is to be invited into your space, or they might want you to go with them.

If by strength of will, or by sheer luck you manage to refuse to comply with their initial wishes and retreat back into your car or the safety of your house, you will slowly feel a sense of security returning to you, (and so you should, you have just had the nearest escape of your life).

Sometimes, after being refused the BEK or BEP will simply vanish into thin air, or run away at an impossibly fast pace; sometimes if you're really unlucky, they will chase after you.
Who are they and what do they want? You would be forgiven for asking. The answer to this is complicated and varied, however, to keep it simple; it seems that they are not human, (some believe they are reptoid in their origins), and their purpose is to cleanse the planet of weak and vulnerable souls, by stealing them and consuming their energy to sustain their own existence.

Once a victim as been robbed of their soul they are left as lifeless shell whose only purpose is to slavishly comply with whatever the black eyed people require of them.
Finally, it is worth noting that there is no known human medical condition that accounts for jet black eyes of this kind.
After reading this short article, I leave the choice of believing or not to you, however, no one could blame you, if on Halloween, you hear the knock on your door and find a child standing there, you take a well advised moment to consider you're trick or treat options carefully.

BUSTED!

Revealing the fakes!

People out there find the need to fake ghost pictures and videos, which makes the job of real paranormal investigators very hard,

We at project-reveal have had over 800+ ghost pictures sent through in 2012 – 2013 to date, from all over the world.

Here is a few we busted to be fake with the help of our fans and public! So watch out for these pictures!

date:
2013-04-01

Your Email Address:
PRIVATE

Your Name.:
Qadeer Ahmed

Picture Description:
My wife usually used to complain of feeling unusual things
since we moved into this villa 8 months back in Ras Al
Khaimah UAE, recently she was complaining of
hearing whispers and steps in the house which I never believed.
Although I am interested in Ghost studies but never faced
anything unusual in my life other than seeing pictures of ghost
some real and some manipulated.. last week while
my wife was clicking her picture from her Mobile(HTC_One)
and watching them on the screen, she mistakenly pressed the
button while the mobile was on the curtains opposite her, to her
surprise she saw this white figure of a girl 120cm
standing in the picture.. I am sure this seems like a manipulated
picture but it is not and still the picture is in her mobile with the
metadata and the sequence what she clicked the picture.. I was
shocked too seeing a picture which I always used to see on the
net and thought that it can be faked.. but this time it is
real right in front of me. if required I can forward the actual
picture with higher resolution.. Please note also that this can't
be a double exposure as she does not resembles anyone in our
family or anyone we know

Read more:
http://ghostsightings.proboards.com/thread/15/white-
ghost#ixzz2emklXhaJ

The Undeparted team

I'm sorry but I had to put my skeptical hat on......
I didn't believe it to be a genuine picture. Obviously this is my opinion only as I'm going off a low res version. But if you look at it the actual photo itself is not great quality, it's quite blurry when you look at details however the "spirit" has a very crisp face despite the fact it's transparent. You can clearly make out the mouth, nose, eye sockets etc.

So due to this I googled "ghost indian girl" and found this webpage:
www.hauntedhovel.com/picture-of-indian-girl-ghost.html

Although it was a small picture, I cut the "ghost" and enlarged it to the same size of the "ghost" in this image, it is extremely pixilated however it appears to be the same "ghost", especially when you look at the way the hair falls on the chest. I also overlapped the images and faded between the 2, this showed that they were pretty much the same image (as stated, i can only find a smaller version of it). I have attached the photos I was working from, the one at the bottom is the actual image size of the second "ghost", you can still see the resemblance.

So in my opinion, unless 2 people photographed the same ghost in the exact same pose, they were using an app! I know its quite pedantic of me but like the saying goes "if its true good to be true, it usually is" and I don't like it when people fake pictures and try to pass them off as real.......

Date:
2013-07-05

Your Email Address:
PRIVATE

Your Name.:
Joaquin Ipince López

Picture Description:
Hey guys.. this picture was taken about a week ago, inside a hospital room. The picture was taken using a Samsung cellphone. Both the baby, the lady holding him , and the lady that took the picture are my relatives. The lady holding the baby told my mother two weeks ago that she always have problems with ghosts, that they bother her, even hurt her. Ok, so ... this picture shocked my family! After the lady saw it she speaking with a priest to protect her.. Most of my family now is scared of her.. And we are trying to be sure that this picture actually isn`t fake. It has to be one of the best ghost pictures i have ever seen, can't believe that it happened to someone close to me. Please analyze it!!
And let me know the answer, it would be really helpful. I know that there are apps for Android where you can add a ghost picture on top of the original.....
That is the only reasonable explanation that i can think of, but my aunt who took the picture claims that it is impossible, that nobody used the cellphone but her. I have modified the contrast, brightness, opacity, etc on Photoshop to get a better look and the ghost, and it doesn´t look fake to me.
Im sending you guys the original picture! Hope you like it (weird) and help us find an
answer to this situation. Thanks!

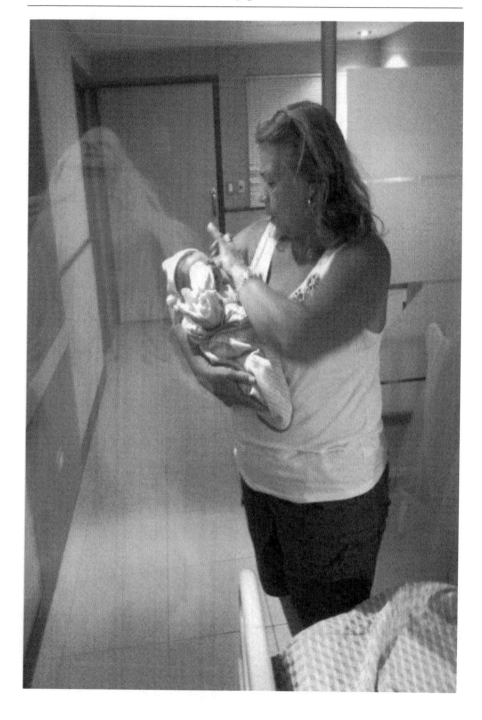

The person who sent it said they were scared of the woman and the spirits following her so I had a look into it and I cannot lie, I didn't believe it was a genuine.

I'm sorry to say guys, its an iphone app

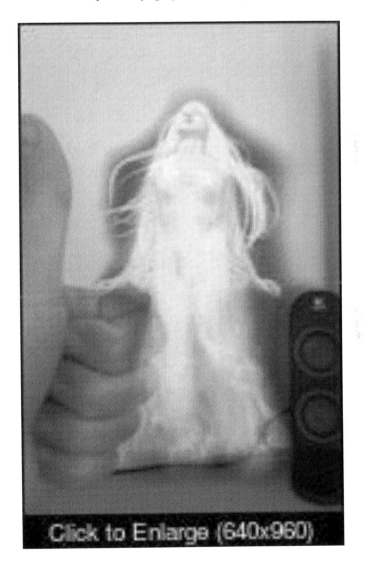

SMETHWICK BATHS HAUNTINGS

Birmingham Smethwick Baths was inbuilt 1933 and was originally referred to as Thimblemill Baths. The building became the native purpose for the general public because the native pool, before it had been then used throughout the war. The building was used as a treatment space for the wounded and therefore the sick Associate in Nursingd its intensive cellars were used as an raid shelter. These areas were additionally wont to store the bodies of these World Health Organization were killed throughout the bombings.

The tunnels below the building additionally hold stories of interrogation of prisoners because the United States Air Force were stationed simply round the corner. Posters that area unit lost in time from the war will still be seen on a number of the walls of the dark subways.

During the 1950's and 1960's the pool was drained and therefore the space was used for concerts and vie host to a number of the foremost illustrious bands, as well as The World Health Organization, The rolling Stones and therefore the rock group. but throughout the 1960's the building gained a name for normal riots that materialized throughout this era.

Smethwick baths is disreputable for its paranormal activity, generally thus alarming that contractors currently refuse to figure at intervals the building.

Smethwick Baths The most haunted a part of the building is underground, within the network of tunnels and cellars that area unit each creepy and disorientating before any mention of the supernatural. Within these subways Associate in nursing tunnels there area unit varied apparitions as well as that of a little boy World Health Organization is seen peering through holes within the wall and a person and kid running to what's urged to be towards a hatchway.

An apparition of a person in a very inexperienced uniform is another regular sight within the subway space. he's typically seen most by folks that have not been within the subways before. throughout a recent public tour the solid apparition of this gentleman was aforementioned to possess walked right passed the cluster at the highest of the tunnel within which all 10 folks within the cluster area unit aforementioned to possess witnessed seeing him.

The underground area once used as a mortuary plays host to a spirit of a person with long hair and beard, World Health Organization has shown himself on many occasions. Meanwhile, within the raid shelter, strange blue lights are seen and infrequently members of employees can enter this space to search out pyramids of stones that are showing neatness engineered on the ground. alittle woman World Health Organization goes by the name of Emily has additionally been gift at intervals this space, typically creating her presence illustrous. In recent years Associate in Nursing escape tunnel was discovered that currently runs beneath a block of flats. One resident of those flats has often seen a trifle woman in her home and it's thought probably that this can be the ghost of Emily too. Shadows and varied figures are seen within the tunnels of Smethwick Baths yet as unexplained sounds and breaths, voices and music that are detected by several guests here too.

Up on the balcony that overlooks the initial pool space is one seat that ne'er remains in Associate in Nursing upright position as a result of a resident spirit which will not tolerate anyone else sitting on the seat. at intervals the dynamic rooms serious footsteps also are detected darting through the building, once there's nobody gift. The lights here area unit on a motion sensing element, nevertheless late they typically start in sequence, as if somebody is walking around, despite the doors being bolted.

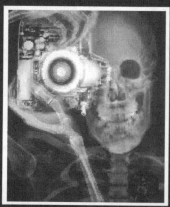

HALLOWEEN AND HOW IT SHOULD BE.

Halloween as provided me with so many memories. Memories of trick and treating, a warm happy house and a tea time meal that I always looked forward to, especially mums home-made parkin. One tradition our family always carried out towards the end of the Halloween night remains an important memory in the fact I have carried it on to this very day.

As a family on Halloween night we would gather round the table maybe with a visiting uncle and aunt and have with us a drink and a small bite to eat. For me this would usually be a glass of milk and a biscuit. We would also bring a photo of a relative we would like to talk about one that may have past away a few years ago but someone would defiantly bring the photo of any family members that may have passed during the last year. I always remember it being a light hearted gathering and as a child it was fun to listen to my mum and dads crazy life stories of some of the relatives. Behind the photo of the relative they would also place a drink for that person usually a favourite drink they knew they liked. This ritual was just something I remember doing as a child and it was always at the end of Halloween night and after everyone had talked about the relative in front of them I would then go to bed. I would always ear the adults talking around the table as I fell asleep.

As I grew older I always had an interest in the human spirit and spirituality not necessarily religion but certain aspects of the soul and the energies provided by the universe. Now this interest was not as strong when I was in my early years but started to come through when I was around 18/19. One set of events in particular I found very interesting and it started when I was moving into my student accommodation. As I moved into my small dwelling the few things I did have I arranged in a way that for some reason reminded me of home like my bedroom and I do remember taking one of my mums ornaments from the living room and placing it in my living quarters, it was like an anchor to remind me of home.

I stayed in my accommodation for 3 years the first year I went home for Halloween but the second things fell funny to a point where I couldn't make it home for the family gathering that they still have to this day. So in my own way I decided to have a little gathering of my own with a few friends I have made at university. We had a few drinks and we all provided some student snacks and I also decided to invite around a medium, its Halloween after all and the other girls thought it was a good idea. The night went well with a few drinks, some food and the lady that came around as a medium had a good light energy about her and her style of giving messages was such that she didn't ask questions she would just give you the message and I would say most of them were very good and precise for that person. The medium also gave us some insight to a few subjects that came up and we found her very helpful. One thing she did do was to draw a few pictures for people as a message. One of those pictures was for me and it was of a lady and she was wearing old style of clothing and she was slightly leaning on my living room bookshelf. There was also a ornament on the window ledge in the drawing and it is nothing I had in the house it was in the shape of a elongated S with a slightly curved line going through it.

A couple of months later my auntie came round to see me which I always looked forward to as we always had interesting conversations. One of the conversations we had was about my interest in spiritualism and certain practices. During this conversation my auntie gave me this book very much like a grimoire that she had compiled with information of family members in the past that had interests in the subject. Now it was an old book but on the first page there was a symbol and I thought I had seen it before and then realised it was the same as the ornament on the drawing the medium had given me. So I showed my auntie the drawing and she was interested to see the symbol but also very interested in the lady leaning on the bookshelf. Now my auntie acknowledged it was a quick sketch of sorts but with the clothes and the hair and basic features of the face she said this looks very much like your great great grandmother. Apparently she had come up in a few messages in the past regarding the subject of spiritualism.

From that night the medium came and gave me that drawing with the lady leaning on the bookshelf with the symbol as an ornament to my auntie arriving a few months later and it all piecing together I find it a bit much for coincidence. For me it was a message something to remind me there's more to life than we sometimes realize. I will always be interested in the subjects of spiritualism and the energies of the soul and with that I will also be researching my great great grandmother. As for the book I was given it now lives in my bookcase in the living room.

Story compiled from source and provided by,

Red Ridge Paranormal.

FRANKS BOX

In 1980, William O'Neil created associate degree electronic audio device known as "The Spiricom."

O'Neil claimed the device was engineered to specifications that he received psychically from Saint George Mueller, a individual United Nations agency had died six years antecedently. At a Washington, DC news conference on April vi, 1982, O'Neil declared that he was ready to hold two-way conversations with spirits through the Spiricom device, and provided the look specifications to researchers for complimentary. However, no one is understood to possess replicated the results O'Neil claimed victimization their own Spiricom devices, O'Neil's partner, retired businessman Saint George Meek, attributed O'Neil's success, and also the inability of others to copy it, to O'Neil's mediumistic talents forming a part of the loop that created the system work.

Another device specifically created in a trial to capture EVP is "Frank's Box" or the "Ghost Box".

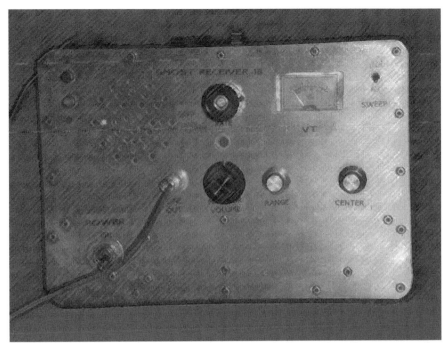

Created in 2002 by EVP enthusiast Frank Sumption for supposed time period communication with the dead, Sumption claims he received his style directions from the mythical place. The device is represented as a mix racket generator and AM wireless changed to comb back and forth through the AM band choosing split-second snippets of sound. Critics of the device say its result is subjective and incapable of being replicated, and since it depends on atmospherics, any significant response a user gets is only coincident, or just the results of pareidolia.

Over the years the franks box has come in many variations, and hacks to make your own simply by cutting a pin,

First Hack

Second Hack

The 12-470 Radio Shack Hack is very difficult to find and one of the first two models of "Shack Hack" ghost boxes discovered.

It comes with a built-in speaker and sweeps the AM or FM band at the perfect speed.

Third Hack

Forth Hack

From now we can expect many more outrageous funky designs with more functions added to help the field of research in the paranormal.

Free Pendulum board

THE PARANORMAL MAGAZINE

VOLUME THREE

LIKE US! ON FACEBOOK

www.facebook.com/theparanormalmagazine

Our New WEBSITE

http://paranormal-magazine.com

<u>WIN A Signed Copy Of Issue 4</u>

Give an honest REVIEW of our book to win the chance to win a signed copy of issue 3.

Please visit amazon.co.uk or .com to write the review about this book.

LEE STEER
AUTHOR – EDITOR

WAYNE RIDSDEL
ILLUSTRATOR, AUTHOR

CO AOUTHORS
PHILIP WILLAIMS
JOHN WILLIAMS

THE PARANORMAL MAGAZINE

A Unique ghost hunting magazine.
Brought to you from the 2 minds of: Lee Steer, Wayne Ridsdel,
With help from Philip & john Williams

The mission is to Educate, and showcase the world of the
paranormal, Featuring Famous Hauntings, A to Z, Ghost Hunting
Equipment's, How to Makes, Myths and legends, Fakes BUSTED,
Old traditions, Ghost Pictures, New Hauntings, and much more..

Thanks for showing an interest in our official paranormal magazine
series
All enquires please email
Asteer8@aol.com

In this ISSUE you get a free Pendulum Board cutout.

HAPPY CHRISTMAS

CONTENTS
A TO Z
G, H, I

-

CHRISTMAS SANTAS DARK HELPER

-

BORLEY RECTORY PART 3

-

VAMPIRISM

-

HAUNTED HERITAGE
BOSWORTH BATTLEFIELD
DONINGTON LE HEATH MANOR HOUSE
SNIBSTON DISCOVERY PARK

-

IN THE DEAD OF NIGHT

-

GHOST PICTURES

-

HAUNTED I PHONES

-

DEMONOLOGY

-

LEYLINES

-

WHY TURN OUT THE LIGHTS

-

HOW TO USE AN OUJIA BOARD SAFELY

-

SMART PHONES ARE HAUNTED

-

A TO Z

In each issue we cover 3 letters from the a to z, this issue we will cover
G, H, I

Geo Phone

Geo phones are cool pieces of ghost hunting equipment; it is designed to
pick up on seismic vibrations, below the earth's surface.
It is made up of a seismic sensor and a light display

When you combine both together with power, casing, and toggle
switch it can look something like this.

The idea is to place this object within a room were footsteps are heard, ideally with a camera facing the geo. These are very sensitive devices, and will pick up the slightest tap.

The more dominant the tap the more lights will show which indicate strength of the vibration.

Haunted

Haunted is a term which is used a lot within the paranormal community, 1 in 10 people believe that they have a haunted house, which is a very high figure, I personally have attended many claims of haunted houses in the uk and found that over 50% of the houses we visit are in fact new builds. So in reality old houses aren't just haunted, it poses another question maybe it's the person who's haunted!

If someone says they are haunted it normally means that they are tormented by a spirit ghost, on a regular basis.

The typical haunted house reports the following

Objects been moved
Shadows seen
Strange smells
Small circles of light appear
Feelings of been touched at night
Light turning off
TV turning on
Sounds heard.

If you feel you are troubled by a ghost, first thing to do is not panic, and try to accept it, and ask the spirit to stop or go away. Many people really don't like to talk about these issues, as they feel they will be judged, but a thing to remember is you are not alone, 1000s of people will be experiencing the exact same thing.

If you feel you would like an expert to check out your property then please email asteer8@aol.com and we will try to find answers on why this is happening.

Infrasound

Infrasound is a low frequency sound wave, which cannot be picked up by the human earing range which is 20 Hz – 20.000 Hz.
Infra sound is 0 – 20 Hz.

So what does this have to do with the paranormal?
Infrasound is small vibrations of sounds which travel through objects, and infrasound may be the main cause for EVPS, "electronic voice phenomena" which is believed to be ghosts speaking through electronic devices.

For example you investigate a house which is very close to a water fall, You set a voice recording going, and on the reply you notice a strange growl sound. This could very well be the vibrations carried through the rock work right to your recorder.

Infra sound can also explain why some objects can move and fall. As the vibrations carry the object of the edge.

So my tip would be to take a note of your surroundings, and list possible interactions before you even start an investigation.

CHRISTMAS – SANTA'S DARK HELPER.

For as long as I can remember my family have always started the Christmas decorations on the 6th of December. I never thought of why that particular date the 6th of December but just recently I have stumbled on why. The 6th of December happens to be Saint Nicolas Day. Traditionally on this day St Nicolas would leave gifts in children's shoes. Apparently gifts would be traded on this day in some countries. Now even though we trade gifts on a different day maybe starting the decorations on this day is just a good way to mark the big mans birthday.

Now we have just spoke of St Nicolas and how he gives presents to the good children of this world and I am sure we have all heard that if your bad you will receive a lump of coal and probably a pear or tangerine. Now what could be more effective would be the following.

As Santa Claus (St Nicolas) is the figure to reward the good children there is a figure that is in charge of punishment. Krampus is a devilish being with the characteristics of an old man crossed with a goat. With long hair and a crooked hunched body he is known to thrash chains and ring a bell looking for the wrong doers he has witnessed through the year.

Now if I was told this guy would be turning up I would have thought twice before being naughty on Christmas Eve, oh well they would have got a day's peace at least.

Krampus dates back with connections to Greek mythology and Norse mythology but has a strong existence in Germanic traditions. The whole recognition of this anti Santa has been one of hot debate in religious and political context. The early Catholic Church did discourage the celebrations of Krampus and during the inquisition extra efforts were placed on stamping them out. In the style of paganism these efforts to stamp out these celebrations did not work as celebrations carried on to the point where in the 17th century the Krampus celebrations were incorporated into Christian winter celebrations by pairing them with St Nicolas. The debates over the acknowledgment of Krampus carried on into the 20th century more so highlighted in Austria when in the 1930`s after the civil war the Krampus tradition was prohibited. Again in the 1950`s in Austria leaflets where handed out that said Krampus was an evil man. And yet again a resurgence of the celebration has surfaced in good old pagan style it always comes back.

Now I have heard a story about Krampus and found it very interesting.

Santa one year was getting very concerned as his naughty list was vastly outweighing his good children list. Coming to the understanding that the threat of a lump of coal was not enough to deter children from doing wrong and his overwhelming kind hearted nature, Santa decided to summon an entity called Krampus. Santa knew that Krampus would watch all the children and if they did wrong Krampus would punish.

All I have to say is we should watch out for Krampus as he maybe visiting us sometime in the future.

Happy Christmas RedRidge X.

LURE OF THE VAMPIRE VAMPIRISM

Wayne Ridsdel

PART ONE

Mention Vampires to anyone now and instantly they will conjure up images…pale complexioned aristocrats, in fine clothes and draped in long, red lined cloaks…hiding fearsome features whilst sulking from shadow to shadow in search of their next victim!

Traditionally, an unsuspecting buxom wench, once bitten by a preying vampire, would spend eternity – neither dead nor alive…but suspended in the dark realms of the 'un-dead'. Her ultimate task…to serve her fiendish master, and entice further victims into the vampire's lair. Her only hope of salvation – the form of a wooden stake – plunged with such ferocity and accuracy, as to penetrate her blackened heart.

As romantic and exciting as the above may sound, it is no more than modern fiction, evolved from the imagination of the famous 19th century, Irish writer Bram Stoker. (8 November 1847-20 April 1912). His devilish Gothic character, 'Count Dracula' was an instant success and has remained a vampire icon for many, (if not most followers) ever since.

This magnificent 'story' is almost entirely responsible for modern media's obsession to present. Its countless variations are the epitome of vampirism, when in fact true vampirism dates back almost to antiquity…prevailing in many cultures and continents throughout the world.

The Druid's embraced it, the Celts, the Romans, and for 300 years it was even included in Christian teachings until the Roman's influence eventually phased it out.

Throughout its passage in time, Vampire Lore has incited scorn, ridicule, disbelief, but always a sense of fear is ignited by its mere mention.

THE ORIGINS OF A DARK CULTURE

VAMPIRISM

Wayne Ridsdel

PART TWO

To trace back to the origins of vampirism we must travel back in time to an era that pre-dates Christianity by over a thousand years. Druids are said to have believed that two of their major Gods of the Harvest were banished into the flames of the sun and destroyed, later to return as vampires.

From this point in time onwards any would be researcher must persist in a journey through an impenetrable fog of fantasy, fiction, folk lore and myths if he or she is to find anything that even resembles a satisfactory answer, let alone a plausible conclusion to this centuries old mystery.

This article does little more than scratch the surface; many more generations of intrepid investigators need to sift out the facts from the fiction.

The purpose of my article is not to foolishly claim I have any answers that warrant credulity in any sense, but to present some of the documented theories into the open – to inspire debate and discussion.

The word 'vampire' (vampir, vampyre) has its origins in Slavonic, but with similarities in: Russian, Polish, Czech, Serbian and Bulgarian. In addition to these similar words can also be found in early Greek, Danish, Swedish and Hungarian languages.

All the above cultures and their respective religions share one common denominator in regard to Sanguinarian Vampirism. The belief that the vampire is an 'undead' creature of either male or female gender, and thirsts for blood to sustain its horrid existence. Another point worthy of note, is that all the cultures listed here hold the firm belief that a Holy or consecrated object will protect any living or dead victim. This belief has survived the rigours of time to such an extent, that in certain areas of Greece it is still customary to place a consecrated object between the lips of a deceased person, or even sew the mouth shut to prevent the entrance or indeed exit of any evil spirit.

There is a school of thought which suggests vampirism was in fact a concept created by the early Roman Catholic church to instil fear into the hearts of the masses, claiming that the only protection against evil – in the form of 'vampires' – lay within the teachings of Christian religions.

It is also worth noting that through various stages of history, the vampire has changed in form and appearance to meet contemporary ideals. Most notable of all being the period prior to the seventeenth century where this dreaded blood thirsty creature gained the ability of shape shifting – ultimately taking on the conveniently menacing shape and habits of the vampire bat. However, when considering this fact the reader should bear in mind that vampires existed long before discovery of this species of bat – native to Central and South America.

In Australia, Native Aborigine's have long held the belief in the power of blood and its effectiveness in curing sickness and giving an ill person more life.

In West Africa and other areas of Africa, blood is revered for its power. If a person sheds blood, it has to be covered, to prevent evil spirits from gorging on it and seeking out the person to whom it belongs. Should it be successful, the spirit may revitalise the body of the dead and destroy the body and soul of the living.

All the above references are in regard, albeit briefly, to Sanguinarian Vampirism. By definition, a creature that gorges and feasts on the blood of humans and animals to sustain its own existence.

Allied to Sanguinarian Vampirism, is the equally ancient belief in the existence of the Psychic Vampire. A culture of vampirism, although less gory, it is if anything, more prevalent in modern society than its bloody counterpart.

(NB: The author would like to add that in no way does he condone the practise of vampirism and points out that practioners of Sanguinarian Vampirism, in modern times also leave themselves prone to diseases such as septicaemia and HIV/AIDS).

VAMPIRES IN MIND
VAMPIRISM

Wayne Ridsdel
PART THREE

Unlike Sanguinarian Vampirism, Psychic, Vampirism differs in one essential aspect; Instead of the insatiable urge to feast on the blood of humans and animals, a psychic vampire is driven to leach the pranic energy, (more popularly known as 'Life Force'), from it's victims.

Although under-going numerous changes in various subcultures throughout history, the psychic predator as always stayed true to its basic origins back in ancient times. And following the teachings of Asetianism.

In 1930, Dion Fortune wrote of psychic parasitism in relation to vampirism, and considered it a combination of psychic and psychological pathology.

The term Psychic Vampire was first used in the 1960's when Anton La Vey, the founder of the Church of Satan coined the term in his highly controversial book, 'The Satanic Bible'. This book began a storm of outrage and ridicule that still rages on in many areas of the world today, and still receives understandable condemnation from all orthodox churches and religions.

The term was also used in Luis Marques's book, 'The Asetian Bible, where he is at pains to point out that, the contemporary psychic vampire's beliefs are based on the esoteric tradition of Asetianism, which relies on predatory spirituality and the extensive use of Ancient Egyptian symbolism whose teachings are strictly and thoroughly maintained by the occultist Order of Aset Ka.

The Modern Day Psychic Vampire:
The majority of so called modern day psychic vampires, are (it seems) No more than individuals who seek to stand out from the masses in bizarre or unconventional dress and tend to follow a conveniently changeable set of morals and ideals. It has to be said that these morals and ideals appear to bare uncanny resemblance to those portrayed in modern media imagery. The sad consequence of this, albeit increasingly popular, subculture is that the original and ancient culture is declining into no more than a modern fashion statement.

This said, there are a surviving minority of Asetian followers who still practise their secret art under a veil of comparative secrecy. They are to be found in small 'cults', world wide, feeding from the psychic energy of not only their own numbers, but also, it is reported from unsuspecting victims.

A psychic vampire does not stand out in a crowd – according to his belief, his or her very survival is dependant on their ability to move around unnoticed. Draining small inconsequential amounts of energy from many victims, leaving them feeling slightly tired and lethargic, but in the main unharmed. The predator is then thought to move on to its next victim, whilst increasing revitalisation by each encounter.

As already mentioned, the psychic vampire shows no outward differences from any other 'normal' human. However, over the years research has shown that individuals claiming to be psychic vampires do display certain psychological traits, not least of all a marked tendency towards schizophrenia.

In conclusion: It has to be said that vampirism and its associate subcultures have survived from the times of antiquity, passing through various phases and fads. We can only hope that if it continues in the current trend, its effect on the public at large will also continue to drift away from the fatal consequences of its original origins and subsequent teachings.

BORLEY RECTORY PART 3

CHRONOLOGY

1863 – 1965

Wayne Ridsdel

Once known as the 'Most Haunted House in England' Borley Rectory has seen many cases of paranormal phenomena over many years. Below is a chronology of some of that phenomena reported by various occupants and subsequent investigators.

It is however, worth remembering that much of the phenomena took place long before the last building was built by Reverend Henry Bull in 1863, though, accurate records of the years prior to 1863 are few and far between, hence I have concentrated on information that can be verified by records in the public domain.

I hope this brief account will serve as a permanent source of useful information for any reader who is interested enough to carry out their own research into the goings-on within this incredible location and the various families who lived and endured untold mysteries.

1863   Borley Rectory constructed by Rev. H.D.E. Bull, rector of Borley.

1875-6   The rectory is extended as the Bull family increases

1881   Harry Price born January 17th.
1892   Henry Bull dies, succeeded by Harry F. Bull.
1900   The four Bull sisters see the Borley nun (28 July) and witness other phenomena.

1911   Reverend Bull marries and moves to Borley Place, Bull sisters remain in the rectory.

1920   Rev. Bull moves back to the rectory.
1920   Harry Price joins the Society for Psychical Research.

1926   Price forms the National Laboratory for Psychical Research, which later becomes the University of London Council for Psychical Investigation.

1927   Harry Bull dies, 9th June. Borley Rectory empty
1928   Rev. G.E. Smith moves takes up residence in October.

1929   Rev Smith contacts Daily Mirror in June and is visited by reporter Mr. V.C. Wall.

1929   First press report 10 June.
1929   Price accompanied by secretary Miss Kaye) visits rectory for first time 12th June. Various phenomena experienced.

1929   Price and others visit rectory unusual phenomena experienced 27 June.

1929   Price, Miss Kaye and Lord Charles Hope visited rectory more phenomena reported 5th July.

1929   Smith leaves the rectory 14 July.
1929   Price, Miss Kaye and Charles Sutton (reporter) visit around 25 July.

1929   Lord Hope, Miss Kaye and others visit, Price absent due to illness 28/29 July.

1930   Smiths leave Borley and move to Norfolk.
1930   Re. L.A. Foyster with wife Marianne and 2 year old child Adelaide move into rectory 16th October.

1930/1   Rev Foyster keeps a record of phenomena.
1931   Sir George and Lady Whitehouse visit with son Richard and form view that Marianne is responsible for the phenomena August.

1931   Bull sisters ask Price to visit rectory again. 29 September.

1931   Rev Foyster invites Price, 1st October.
1931   W.H. Salter of the SPR visits rectory and advises Rev Foyster to deter Price from visiting or demands that he promises in writing that he will not seek any form of publicity relating to the rectory. 9th October.

1931   Price, Mrs Goldney and others visit. Price suspects Marianne of deception and leaves on bad terms with the Foysters.

1931   Richard Whitehouse visits the Smiths in Norfolk. December.

1932   Price mentions in a letter to Rev Smith that he would like to visit Borley, but the Foysters will not agree. 8th January.

1932   Price visits rectory, reason unknown. April November.

1933-4   Marianne Foyster working in London, home at weekends Price states his views about Marianne in a letter to Edward Fielding, he adds, five years ago the place was literally alive with – something.

1935   Price makes a BBC broadcast about Borley rectory.

1935   Foysters leave Borley rectory unoccupied. October

1936   Confessions of a ghost hunter published February.

1936   Rev A.C. Henning new rector of Borley resides at Liston

1936   Rev Guy L' Estrange makes a BBC broadcast about Borley rectory, December.

1937   Price rents rectory for one year, he enroles 48 others to help investigate Borley rectory phenomena. S.H. Glanville assists Price in supervision of investigation.

1937   Price makes a BBC broadcast about Borley rectory.

1937-8   Glanville's daughter uses a séance to investigate Borley further.

1938   In a séance the rectory is threatened with destruction by fire, 27 March.

1938   Price and investigators move out on 19 May.
1938   Captain Gregson purchases rectory intending to capitalise on its reputation, December.

1938   Price makes a BBC broadcast about Borley rectory.

1939   Captain Gregson makes a BBC broadcast about Borley rectory.

1939   Price meets with Whitehouses and changes his view of Mrs Foyster's involvement. Price and Foyster on cordial terms once again. April.

1939-44   Dr A.J.B. Robertson and others make numerous visits to ruins of rectory and submit a report to Price later published in the End of Borley Rectory.

1940   Rev. G.E Smith dies same day as the Most Haunted House in England is published on 3rd August.

1940   Many people contact Price describing unexplained phenomena at rectory site.

1941   Price makes a BBC broadcast about Borley Rectory.

1943   Polish officers visit Borley on 28 June and 28 July.

1943   Price conducts excavation of Rectory wells and cellars. Finds include human bones, 17th August.

1944   Ruins of rectory demolished.
1944   Price with Cynthia Ledsham of 'Time Left, magazine visit during demolition work, 'flying brick photographed 5th April.

1945   In a letter to the Church Times' Mrs Smith denies she or the Rev Smith ever believed the rectory to be haunted. Price, Henning and Glanville puzzled by this. October.

1945   Poltergeist over England published, containing a chapter about Borley Rectory.

1946   Price with others makes a BBC broadcast about Borley rectory.

1947   Price with others makes a BBC broadcast about Borley rectory

1948   Harry Price dies whilst writing a third Borley Book, 29th March.

1948   Mrs Smith repeats her disbelief of Borley hauntings in a letter to the Daily Mail. 26 May

1948   Reporter Charles Sutton writing in the Inky Way Annual accuses Price of manufacturing phenomena on their visit in 1929 December.

1954   Mr S.H. Glanville dies.

1956   The Haunting of Borley rectory – A Critical Survey of the evidence by E.J. Dingwall. K.M. Goldney and T.H. Hall published.

1965   An examination of the Borley Report by Robert J. Hastings published March.

HAUNTED HERITAGE
BOSWORTH BATTLEFIELD

BOSWORTH
BATTLEFIELD HERITAGE CENTRE
AND COUNTRY PARK

The History of Bosworth Battlefield

The Battle of Bosworth (or Bosworth Field) was the last significant battle of the <u>Wars of the Roses</u>, the <u>civil war</u> between the <u>Houses of Lancaster</u> and <u>York</u> that raged across England in the latter half of the 15th century. Fought on 22 August 1485, the battle was won by the Lancastrians. Their leader <u>Henry Tudor, Earl of Richmond</u>, by his victory became the first English monarch of the <u>Tudor dynasty</u>. His opponent, <u>Richard III</u>, the last king of the House of York, was killed in the battle. Historians consider Bosworth Field to mark the end of the <u>Plantagenet dynasty</u>, making it a defining moment of English and Welsh history.

Richard's reign began in 1483 when he was handed the throne after his twelve-year-old nephew Edward V, for whom he was acting as Lord Protector, was declared illegitimate and ineligible for the throne. The boy and his younger brother disappeared in mysterious circumstances, and Richard's support was eroded by rumours of his involvement in the death of his wife. Across the English Channel in Brittany, Henry Tudor, a descendant of the greatly diminished House of Lancaster, seized on Richard's difficulties to challenge for and claim to the throne. Henry's first attempt to invade England was frustrated by a storm in 1483, but at his second attempt he arrived unopposed on 1 August 1485 on the southwest coast of Wales. Marching inland, Henry gathered support as he made for London. Richard mustered his troops and intercepted Henry's army south of Market Bosworth in Leicestershire. Thomas, Lord Stanley, and Sir William Stanley brought a force to the battlefield, but held back while they decided which side it would be more advantageous to support.

Richard divided his army, which outnumbered Henry's, into three groups (or "battles"). One was assigned to the Duke of Norfolk and another to the Earl of Northumberland. Henry kept most of his force together and placed it under the command of the experienced Earl of Oxford. Richard's vanguard, commanded by Norfolk, attacked but struggled against Oxford's men, and some of Norfolk's troops fled the field. Northumberland took no action when signalled to assist his king, so Richard gambled everything on a charge across the battlefield to kill Henry and end the fight. Seeing the king's knights separated from his army, the Stanleys intervened; Sir William led his men to Henry's aid, surrounding and killing Richard. After the battle, Henry was crowned king below an oak tree in nearby Stoke Golding, now a residential garden.

Henry hired chroniclers to portray his reign favourably; the Battle of Bosworth was popularised to represent the Tudor dynasty as the start of a new age. From the 15th to 18th centuries the battle was glamorised as a victory of good over evil. The exact site of the battle is disputed because of the lack of conclusive data, and memorials have been erected at different locations. The Bosworth Battlefield Heritage Centre was built, in 1974, on a site chosen based on a theory that has since been challenged by several scholars and historians. In October 2009, a team of researchers, who had performed geological surveys and archaeological digs in the area from 2003, suggested a location two miles (3 km) southwest of Ambion Hill.

What does Bosworth Battlefield have to offer as a paranormal venue?

With the recent discovery and confirmation of Richard III's body in Black Friars in Leicester, Bosworth Battlefield is now a top visitor attraction. Haunted Heritage have exclusive rights to conduct paranormal walks using ghost detection equipment at Bosworth and are able to get closer to the actual battle field than most of the general public are allowed.

The evening begins with a meet and greet session and group members being introduced to and informed about the 'ghost' detection equipment available. Group members are able to use dousing rods, EMF meters and ghost boxes (record voice phenomena) to capture anything that goes 'bump' in the night!

The paranormal 'ghost' walk will take you to Albion Hill, Shenton Station and the edge of the battlefield and then through the woods to the old well where Richard III is thought to have taken his last drink. Haunted Heritage's medium will draw on any spirits or residual energy present as well as retell stories of recorded sightings and phenomena previously witnessed. In collaboration with this, the Bosworth guide and historian will talk you through the events as they unfolded at the Battle of Bosworth and verify any phenomena witnessed.

DONINGTON LE HEATH MANOR HOUSE

Where is Donington Le Heath Manor House?

Donington le Heath Manor House Museum is a surviving example of a manor house built around seven hundred years ago in Donington le Heath, near the town of Coalville, Leicestershire. It was once owned by a relative of one of the Gunpowder plotters, and is now managed by Leicestershire County Council.

The History of Donington Le Heath Manor House

The museum is based in a medieval manor house, believed to date back to 1280. From the style of the architecture of the parts of the building and from tree-ring dating of some of the timbers still present, the present house at Donington was probably built between 1288 and 1295.

Some of the features of the house along with tree-ring dating of the timbers in the roof show that the Manor House was heavily modernized around 1618. It appears that at this time, the downstairs storerooms were converted into a kitchen and a parlor. A new roof was put on and the rooms upstairs were remodeled with a new internal staircase. Externally, the most obvious addition from this period are the large rectangular mullioned windows. At this time, the house was probably owned by John Digby, whose elder brother, Everard Digby was a close friend of Guy Fawkes and was executed in 1606 for his part in the Gunpowder Plot.

From 1670 to 1960, the house was rented out as a tenant farm and Leicestershire County Council bought the Manor House in 1965 to preserve the building for future generations. The Manor House was opened as a museum in 1973.

The Gunpowder Plot

Donington le Heath Manor House was owned, during the 15th and 16th Century, by the Digby family. Sir John Digby fought at the Bosworth Battlefield in 1485 for Henry Tudor. When Henry defeated King Richard III and became King Henry VII he would have rewarded his supporters and it may be the case that he gave back the lands that the Digbys had lost in 1462 for their opposition to the previous kings. During 1574, the property was owned by Everard Digby. Everard was a close friend of Guy Fawkes and he was executed in 1606 for being one of the Gunpowder Plotters.

What does Donington Le Heath Manor House have to offer as a paranormal venue?

Donington Le Heath manor House is steeped in history. It is charming and quaint whilst being remarkably eerie. Haunted Heritage are privileged to have exclusive use of Donington Le Heath as a paranormal venue. The house, barn and gardens offer a range of exciting and different paranormal experiences. Haunted Heritage will guide you to carry out investigations in some of the following areas:

The Tithe Barn, The Gardens, The Old Kitchen, The Old Dairy Room, The Great Hall and the bedroom containing Richard III's bed. Group members will have the opportunity to use a comprehensive range of paranormal investigative equipment such as dousing rods, EMF meters, 'Ghost Boxes' (record voice phenomena) as well as participate in séances, glass deviation and table deviation sessions.

All of our paranormal events to date at Donington Le Heath have been hugely successful with an amazing amount of paranormal activity. We have experienced light phenomena, orbs, poltergeist activity, brilliant voice phenomena, glass deviation, vigorous table deviation, dramatic changes in temperature, distinct readings and spirit communication on EMF meters and with the use of dousing rods to name just a few.

SNIBSTON DISCOVERY PARK

Where is Snibston Discovery Museum?

Snibston is a former coal mining village in Coalville, north west Leicestershire, in the East Midlands. The area is now dominated by the Snibston Discovery Museum, built on the site of the former colliery and consisting of an award-winning interactive museum, scheduled ancient colliery buildings, the Century Theatre, and a 100-acre (0.40 km2) country park and nature reserve. It is located within the National Forest.

The History of Snibston.

Snibston Colliery was one of three coal mines sunk in the 1820s and 1830s that helped create the town of Coalville in north-west Leicestershire. Snibston Colliery was created by the famous engineers George and Robert Stephenson and produced coal continuously from 1833 to 1983. When it finally closed in 1985, the site was bought by Leicestershire County Council with the aim of preserving the most important buildings, turning the rest of the derelict site into a recreational area and building a major new museum of science and working life. The Discovery Park opened in 1992.

Snibston Colliery's railway is one of the earliest ever built in Britain. It was constructed by Robert Stephenson between 1833 and 1836 to connect the colliery with the <u>Leicester and Swannington Railway</u>, built by his father <u>George Stephenson</u> on the east side of Coalville. This railway was created to carry coal, not passengers. After Snibston Colliery closed in 1983 the railway line was partially dismantled and abandoned. However the section of line from the mine to the centre of Coalville was restored between 1998 and 2001.

Many of the historic mining buildings are now very rare survivals of this once-widespread industry and have been designated as <u>scheduled ancient monuments</u> by the Government.

The Century Theatre

The Century Theatre or 'the Blue Box' is a portable theatre, built on a series of ex-RAF trailers in 1952. The theatre was designed by John Ridley who used ingenious design; an aluminum superstructure and hydraulic rams, to create a professional quality theatre building that could be folded up and moved by road.

Following its opening night in Hinckley in September 1952, the theatre toured Britain until 1974, remaining only a few weeks in each venue. From 1974 until 1997 the Century was used as the town theatre of Keswick in Cumbria, and then, thanks to support from the Heritage Lottery Fund, it was saved from the scrapyard, refurbished and brought home to Leicestershire.

The theatre was run by its own company expressly created to take quality drama to communities throughout Britain and helped greatly with post-war cultural reconstruction. Many of the company's actors and technicians went on from touring with the Century to make important contributions to theatre in Britain and abroad.

What does Snibston Discovery Park have to offer as a paranormal venue?

Snibston is an amazing venue to conduct paranormal investigations as it has a wide range of varied locations on site that we have access to. Locations that are frequently used to conduct our investigations are:

The Century Theatre, The Fashion Gallery, The Transport and Engineering Gallery, The Locomotive Work Sheds, The Old Pit Top Shaft Entrance, The Miners Lamp Room and Control Room, The Original Colliery Offices and Moody's Wheelwright and Undertakers Workshops.

All off these locations have demonstrated varied levels and different types of paranormal activity on a frequent basis. Members of our investigation groups have witnessed light phenomena, orbs, poltergeist activity, voice phenomena, glass deviation, table deviation, dramatic changes in temperature, distinct readings and spirit communication on EMF meters to name just a few.

Our medium and has communicated with spirits that date as far back as 1218 up to the present day.

IN THE DEAD OF NIGHT

Wayne Ridsdel

Regardless of whether one accepts the medical explanation, or the paranormal theory for this surprisingly common condition, there is no escaping the fact that it is a terrifying experience for the sufferer.

Sleep paralysis is closely related to the natural paralysis occurring in the REM (Rapid Eye Movement) state of sleep. The victim is fully conscious and alert, yet the body remains paralyzed. In this state, the brain is capable of manifesting intensely vivid hallucinations, which the body cannot react to. The understandable reaction to this scenario is fear and panic. To the sufferer, the experience is horrifyingly real. All the natural senses of the individual remain fully functioning, i.e. smell, taste, touch, hearing, and sight are all present and only add to the horror.

During REM sleep the body's metabolism is slowed down, the heart rate is lowered, as too is blood pressure and respiratory rate. Along with this comes muscle paralysis; all these adaptations are a safety mechanism to prevent injury during the dreaming state. Without this natural defense, the individual could thrash out with limbs and enact their dreams.

With a reduced heart beat and respiratory rate the victim will experience the feeling of pressure on the chest wall and a difficulty in breathing. In this natural state of fear and panic, the victim may well interpret this sensation as some kind of weight on his/her chest.

Some victims of this horrifying condition are able to convince themselves that the experience was no more than a dream – a nightmare at worst. Others remain convinced they have been attacked by some kind of supernatural entity. The latter are adamant their assailant is an external reality and not a product of their subconscious. However, sleep specialists and psychologists dismiss this by explaining that thoughts, images, and sensations released from an individual's subconscious are all ultimately alien to the individual. This area is a vast storeroom for random psychological phenomena, which the conscious brain either cannot, or will not analyse and accept as reality. Hence, the victim concludes that all the hallucinatory elements of a sleep paralysis attack are received from an external source.

Throughout the world and the passing of time, the above physiological aspects of sleep paralysis have been and remain the same, regardless of the victim's race, religion, or culture. It is the almost countless interpretations of these symptoms, which make sleep paralysis one of, if not the most common and feared paranormal phenomena.

It is beyond the scope and capability of this article and its author to cover all the physiological and psychological aspects of sleep paralysis. Therefore, I have elected to turn my attention to offering the reader a brief overview of the many variations and interpretations of the occult aspects of this fascinating and terrifying phenomenon.

THE DARKER SIDE OF THE NIGHT

Frank De Felitta's novel, 'The Entity' which was subsequently made into a very successful horror movie was in fact based on the alleged true story of Carlotta Moran, a young Californian woman. Her terrifying ordeal from the 1970s is supported by psychiatric reports and physical evidence in the form of bruises to her body. Some researchers claim that Carlotta was attacked by a non-physical male entity known as an Incubus, (female counterpart, Succubus).

There are several excellent books and papers available on sleep paralysis. 'Creatures from Inner Space' (Stan Gooch) and 'The Flying Cow' (Guy Lyon Playfair), and 'The Terror that comes in the Night' (David J. Hufford) are just three examples.

SLEEP PARALYSIS IN FOLKLORE:

The following list is a brief summary of various perceptions of sleep paralysis in some cultures throughout the world:

African culture describes sleep paralysis as 'The Witch Riding Your Back'.

Cabbodian, Laitian, and Thai culture believe sleep paralysis to be 'Pee Umm' and Khmout Sukkhot'. These describe dreams of ghostly figures holding down their victims, or merely being nearby. Both terms should not be confused with 'Pee Khao' and 'Khamout Jool' which refers to a ghost possession.

Hmong culture refers to sleep paralysis as 'Dab Tsog' or 'Crushing demon' In this instance the victim claims to see small child-sized entities sitting on their chests.

Many Americam Hmong, (mainly male) have died in their sleep, prompting the Centres for Disease Control to adopt the term, 'Sudden Unexpected Nocturnal Death Syndrome', or (SUNDS).

Viatnamese culture refer to sleep paralysis as 'Ma De', meaning (held down by a ghost or, 'Bong De', (held down by a shadow'.

Chinese culture believes it to be, 'Pinyin; gui y ashen' or 'Pinyin gui ya chan'. Translated: 'Ghost pressing on bed'.

Japanese culture, as 'Kanashibari', meaning (bound or fastened in metal).

Hungarian culture folklore refers to sleep paralysis as 'Lidercnymias'. (Lideric pressing). Here the term can relate to a number of supernatural entities like 'Lideric' (Wraith). 'Boszorkany' (Witch). 'Tunder' (Fairy) or 'Ordogszereto' (Demon Lover). The word 'Boszorkany' stems from the Turkish root 'Bas' meaning (to press).

Icelandic culture refers to sleep paralysis as having a 'Mara' (Devil that sits on one's chest at night).

Malta culture attributes sleep paralysis to an attack by the 'Haddiela' who is the wife of 'Hares'. To help prevent such an attack Maltese people believe to rid themselves of Haddeila, they must place a piece of silverware or a knife under the pillow prior to sleep.

Kurdish culture believes it to be 'Mattaka'. Kurdish people believe the form of a ghost or evil spirit visits them in the night and suffocates them if they have done something bad.

New Guinnea culture, as 'Suk Ninmyo'. Here the origin is from sacred trees that use human essence to sustain their lives. These trees feed on human essence during the night so as not to disturb the human's daily life.

Turkish culture, as 'Karabasan', (The dark presser/assailer).

Mexican culture refer to sleep paralysis as 'Se me Subio el Mureto' (The dead person got on me).

Southern American culture refers to the phenomenon as a 'hag' and it is believed to be a sign of an approaching tragedy or accident.

Southwest Nigeria culture describes sleep paralysis as 'Ogun Oru' (Nocturnal Warfare).

Pakistani culture refers to the phenomenon as encounters with evil jinns and demons. They believe the experience to be the result of enemies performing black magic.

Korean culture, as 'Ga-ui-nool-lim' menaing (pressed by a nightmare).

Tamail and Sri Lankan cultures refer to sleep paralysis as 'Amuku Be' or Amuku Pei' meaning (the ghost that forces one down).

Malay culture, as 'Kena Tindih' meaning (being pressed).

Newfoundland culture refers to the phenomenon as the 'Old Hag'. It is believed that the Hag can be summoned to attack a third party, like a curse. David J. Hufford stated in his 1982 book, 'The Terror That Comes in the Night' that believers call up the Hag by reciting the Lord's Prayer backwards.

Because of the complexity and the profound effect this phenomenon can have on many people's lives I intend to return to this topic in future articles when information from reliable sources becomes available.

SMART PHONES ARE HAUNTED TO

I finally got a smartphone in August and nothing of note happened until now. I'd gotten the usual texts and phone calls for the previous number's owner (I don't do contract phones, it's an AT&T gophone) but tonight at 6:16 pm, as I was sitting in the car, I got a notification from my calendar. It said from 6:25-7:25 pm. I called.

I was confused as to why "I called" was on the calendar… I did not put it there. We concluded that it was from my husband's dad, he had been thinking about him lately and about the fact that his dad had tried to call him right before he died. (My husband's vonage phone was on the fritz and he never got the call). I opened the event and wrote a note back in the description area of the event and saved it. At 7:16pm I got a second notification that also said, "I called." I left the event on instead of dismissing it to see if we get any more notes from it. If we do, I will update.

HOW TO USE A OUIJA BOARD SAFELY

http://divinewisdomforyou.wordpress.com / Submitted

The Ouija Board has been used for many years and the curiosity continues. I would advise you not to use the Ouija Board. When used, it becomes a portal for any entity to come in. It is a very dangerous tool to use if you do not know what you are doing. Even if you do know what you are doing you may come in contact with a negative energy. I have never used one because being a psychic, it's more favorable for me to receive messages through my abilities instead of the Ouija. However, if you do want to use one here are some safety tips.

- Never use it alone
- Make sure that you and the others involved with you are serious about the Ouija and do not look at it as frivolous entertainment.
- Use sage to smudge your place
- Say a prayer (any prayer that involves God entity)for protection and envision a shield of protection that surrounds you and the participants
- Do not ask a question like when will I die or another person die
- You may have to wait about 15 minutes to make contact
- Make circles with the planchette if there is no contact in 15 minutes and wait again
- Do not use mind altering drugs or alcohol when using the Ouija
- Do not use if you or someone else has a psychosis or psychological disorder
- Do not use if you or others have nervous tendencies, are anxious or have addictions
- Sit at a table and do not cross your legs. This allows your energy to flow freely.
- Have someone use pen and paper to write down what a spirit says

- Make sure that the spirits communicate only through the board
- Ask if it is a negative or positive spirit. They will answer you. If it is a negative spirit, move the planchette to Goodbye, close down the board and try again in 30minutes.
- When beginning to make contact ask if there are any spirits in the room. Disregard tapping and other noises you might hear.
- When receiving an answer to your question, make sure that the letters are visible through the hole. If they aren't ask the spirit to make it clear and visible. Always be polite.
- After you are finished talking with a spirit, thank the spirit/spirits for visiting with you and say Goodbye. The spirit should move the planchette to Goodbye and you may close the board. If the spirit does not move the planchette to Goodbye, then tell the spirit you are finished speaking with them and say Goodbye. If the spirit refuses to leave, then you must move the planchette to Goodbye and firmly say Goodbye and ask the spirit to leave out loud.
- Do not use the board for more than 1 hour and 1/2. To use it for longer may be harmful for you.
- Do eat or drink something after using the Ouija to ground yourself.

If you have any other questions, please feel free to contact me at divinesolitude@hotmail.com

DEMONOLOGY

Demonology is the systematic study of demons or beliefs about demons. It deals both with benevolent beings that have no circle of worshipper and demons that are regarded as spirits. The demons regarded as spirits can belong to spirits recognized as primitive animals, that is to say they may be human or non-human. And also separable souls or discarnate spirits which have never inhabited a body.

Under the heading of demons there are a few classified spirits as believed by the human race.Terms therefore includes:

Angels in the Judeo-Christian tradition that fell from grace.

Human souls regarded as genii or familiars such as receive a **Cult** (e.g., ancestor worship).

Ghosts or other malevolent revenants.

I've compiled 2 demons that are commonly used either in films or recorded exorcisms. One demon that is used extensively is Paimon.

If you take a look at The Goetia: The Lesser Key of Solomon the King, Paimon is one of the Kings of Hell, more obedient to Lucifer than the other kings are and has two hundred (one hundred to other authors) legions of demons under his rule. He has a great voice and roars as soon as he comes up until the conjurer compels him and then he answers clearly the questions he as been asked. When the conjurer invokes this demon he must look towards the northwest. The reason for that is because that's the direction of his house and when Paimon appears he must be allowed to ask what he wishes and be answered, in order to obtain the same from him.

Paimon teaches all arts, philosophy, sciences and secret things. He can reveal all mysteries of the Earth, wind and water, what the mind is, and everything the conjurer wants to know.

Baal in grimoire tradition is said to appear in the forms of a man, cat, toad, or combinations of the later. Curiously placed heads of the three creatures onto a set of spider legs have been documented. The full name "Beelzebub" comes from the words "Ba'al" and "Zebub", which together mean "Lord of the Flies". This King of Demons can make those who invoke him invisible as well as impart wisdom. He can control the weather as was his primary duty back in his days as a god.

As i've heard the expression " you have created your own demons", this makes me think could it be true?. And if so can you repel the demons that are created by yourself or passed by others.

I also think because of the world's population getting bigger and and all the differing energy being passed around should we turn to some spiritual enlightenment maybe to help repel some negative energy. Even better stop as much negative energy being created.

by Philip Williams
http://www.redridge-esp.t83.net/

LEY LINES

Right i will try my best to cover in this article enough information to explain the concept of ley lines.
The reason for my opening line is because this subject is a difficult one at that and i can see it leading to a conclusion based on an opinion. We as a group will investigate any concepts of ley lines that we come across.

Well ley lines they are to some people mystical lines of magical power, lines of earth's natural energy, walkways of the ancients or just don't exist. Either way there are many books, articles and theories about them. It's not just the new age spiritualists and alternate dimensional people that believe or study them. This subject has captured the minds of some of the greatest thinkers of our species, Newton and Tesla been two of them.

When it comes to Tesla he believed in a energy grid of the planet. Yes this was a grid of natural energy that could be captured and used by us as a clean energy. Let's say this is correct then maybe the ancients picked up on this and followed these lines of energy to survive. They say flowing water is energy, lines of limestone, animals following certain paths to survive.

Lets say the lines of certain materials within the ground create a lower resistance acting then as a conductor for the earths energy.

My first personnel thought to this after studying acupressure was this could be compared to the acupressure points of the body. Its the same principle, the body has been found to have fibrous tissue with a low resistance and these act as paths for our body to conduct energy from certain points (this also explains chakra points). Already we are covering so many ideas it could be easy to get lost in confusion, i will make some quick bullet points of what i have found.

•   Ley lines are the alignment of megalithic, monuments and places of particular interest. Some say these lines are man made lines of power using stones rocks and other objects to direct power or amplify.

•   Curry lines are lines of the earths natural radiation, some say detectable with dowsing rods and picking the right spot and living in the right line of radiation could be beneficial for ones life. Like all things in nature the wrong spot can be harmful.

•   Black lines have been described has a depressive negative energy. These can be in buildings as a mist or fog or line.

•   Hartmann lines these been more complicated. These are more magnetic in nature with a grid over the planet. The zones in between these lines that push up from the earths surface are localized environments. These environments are said to be delicate to the seasons and hours of the day.

So from the simple concept of ley lines we know they are many lines with different given names.

What if all these lines and all these concepts were seen as one by the people of the past.

I believe there is something in this and there is no reason for the planet not to have channels of energy.
In the end when you have a wealth of energy or water it always finds the easiest way of flowing.
Why should it be any different for the earth's natural energy that it creates on a daily basis.

Please if you have any information on the above topics please let us know, we will appreciate it.
Our aim with this is to gather a well formed theory and practice.

We would also be interested in the detection of these lines, the relationship with crystals, locations and how to use these lines.
I understand from an email that obelisks were used to draw power from the earth and also heal weak points of the earths energy. It said light objects (light been classed as under 800lbs) are placed on energy upshoots to help gather energy for use and direction, this is done in locations where the earths energy is healthy and plentiful.
Heavy objects over 800lbs are placed on energy down shoots to place energy into the earth where its weak and sparse.

Below are some bullet points i have gathered for the information i have so far,

•   the planet as a wealth of energy, in some areas more concentrated than others

- like all collections of   energy it moves in the easiest ways of least resistance
- these paths of energy can be classed as ley lines
- the collection or amount of energy like all things need to be balanced
- balancing these energies can be achieved with obelisks and medicine wheels
- balancing can also be achieved with natural mounds and agriculture
- heavy obelisks can create energy down shoots for areas of weak energy
- light obelisks can create energy upshoots for areas of pent up energy

SCHUMANN RESONANCE

Well what we are looking at here is the Schumann Resonance. I did not have a clue what this was about but while researching ley lines i came across this subject.

I will place some bullet points from the ley lines article that may help with this article,

- the planet as a wealth of energy, in some areas more concentrated than others
- like all collections of   energy it moves in the easiest ways of least resistance
- these paths of energy can be classed as ley lines
- the collection or amount of energy like all things need to be balanced
- balancing these energies can be achieved with obelisks and medicine wheels

- balancing can also be achieved with natural mounds and agriculture
- heavy obelisks can create energy down shoots for areas of weak energy
- light obelisks can create energy upshoots for areas of pent up energy

Ok the subject of ley lines was often in line with weird believers that kiss leafs.
But after writing the article and researching ideas from emails kindly provided by our visitors, i have come to a conclusion that ley lines and other lines with similar concepts make sense and could exist.

This article is about the Schumann resonance so lets get to the idea. This resonance that was researched in a big way by Tesla has allot of backers in the science field to the point where i think the following points are facts.

- Schumann Resonance is the Earths natural frequency/resonance
- This frequency is around 7.5Hz
- it relates strongly with lightning
- lightning on other planets may also be detected
- may also be used to detect earthquake patterns
- also to detect water vapor in the atmosphere
- very variable with the times of the day and seasons

So with planet earth having an iron core and rotating molten this creates an electromagnetic field.
The electromagnetic field creates a frequency of 7.5Hz around the surface of the planet.

This frequency will surely have low points and high points and also areas where its blocked and heightened in energy.

What if these factors and the above bullet points explain why the ancients created myths and rituals for certain aspects of nature. Some rituals like spells, prayers or methods of magic been used at certain points of the day/week or year could have been due to the change and recognition of the Schumann resonance. What if the high points and low points were detected by the ancients and thats the reason for worshiping locations and cursed ground, also for the positions for monoliths, monuments and obelisks.

I have found scientific explanations for the Schumann resonance and that in itself surprises me in a great way. It seems very reasonable that lay lines exist and makes me think that the ancients had an heightened sense of natural science.

VORTEXES

Ok so we have had a brief glimpse into the idea of Ley lines and the Schumann resonance.
We have realised that the earth could have lines of energy running through/over it.
These lines would most likely be arranged in a grid over the planet. We have also come across the idea that the earth itself has its own resonant frequency of power. All these things can help, alter, hinder the way we share this planet.

So when i thought of vortexes i first thought of blue shiny things that demons pop out of.

Then shortly after that i thought no theres vortexes like whirlwinds and other clashes in the climate.

Vortexes simply occur when forces of different strength or direction move around each other.
So if ley lines exist or the Schuman resonance then the possibilities of these energies interacting in such a way should be a very reasonable possibility.

The idea is that there are vortexes all around the world in certain areas and points of the planet.
Some of these vortexes go into the earth where the energy is weak and others go into the air where theres a buildup of energy. Below are some bullet points to cover some of the technical information and also mythical information.

- light obelisks can create energy upshoots for areas of pent up energy
- heavy obelisks can create energy down shoots for areas of weak energy
- creating a counter clockwise vortex creates low pressure
- low pressure takes energy down to the earth
- creating a clockwise vortex creates high pressure
- high pressure sends energy into the atmosphere
- knowing this we can create vortexes accordingly to balance areas out.
- High pressure were classed as a male aspect and a negative one at that.
- Low pressure been a female and positive aspect.
- Some say the dark green circles you can find in the grass are results of vortexes

- some say trees growing in a vortex can cause the bark lines to spiral or the trees to twist
    - some trees also twist round each other.

The above points are some of the common views.

This subject i have thought about and at one point while drinking a cup of tea i realized something quite interesting. At the surface of my tea i could see the glistening of the droplets of oil from my milk.
On the surface of my tea i could see that they were a number of vortexes most probably caused by the heat. This also went along with the whole surface rotating. I also noticed fixed vortexes and also mobile ones acting like moving storms. It to me looked like the pasterns of the ever moving planet.

Written by john williams
Redridge co owner

Why do ghost hunters turn off the lights?

Lights out is a common phrase for ghost hunters, but why? Here a statistic gathered by the total of email submissions we have for ghost pictures.

Out of the first 100 pictures sent in, 22 pictures were at night, 78 were in in broad day light. So this is 78% of people capture ghosts on camera through the day.

I myself like to investigate with lights ON, and OFF. I like to see my surroundings, to see if I can see any activity's reported, so in order to investigate you must be able to see, This is where night vision comes into play.

Invisible light to the human eye, but certain camcorder technology can see this light, which enables you to see in total darkness via the camcorder. Ghosts are either described as dark shadows, or white figures which you can just barely see, so using IR light would show any white objects within the room very clear. Night vision is used to see the things we struggle to see.

So turning out the lights helps us to investigate in different spectrums of lights, White and infrared.

But I would stress to every ghost hunter, do not turn out the lights right away try it with the lights on!

GHOST PICTURES

Marybeth Ziegler
Picture Description: This picture was taken in the
ballroom at the Wolf Creek Inn in Wolf Creek,
Oregon. If you look closely at the big white line, you
will see orbs attached to each end of the line.

Your Name.:
T. Anthony

Picture Description:
My mother took this picture a early November this year
at Redondo Beach in Des Moines, WA on a cold cloudy
day. She took a picture of the waves coming to shore.
When she got home to look at her pictures she noticed
this one had distinctive shape that catches your eye
right away almost in the centre of the photo.
When you zoom on the image it seems to look like a face
a Demon, then when you start to look around the picture
you start to see lots of faces. There seems to be women
and children faces some screaming. It's very eerie and
I encourage you to take a look at this and look around
the image to see how many faces you see. Me myself can

see 5 faces but others who have seen the picture say
they see more.

Your Name: Josh

Picture Description:
Taken at the Pennhurst State School and Hospital in PA.

This is my friend taking a picture of himself in one of
the classrooms while I was down the hall exploring. He
says when he took it there
was nothing behind him.

Later that night we went to look at the pictures we took and saw this one. This is clearly a shadow person; it's some kind of demented figure. It's obviously not a mortal being because the arm is transparent. This was quite chilling to find.

Note: He said he felt strange the whole time he was in the building, a "pins and
needles" feeling on his arms. Perhaps this entity was following him.

Upload Your Ghost Picture:

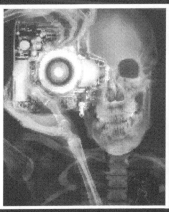

33052788R00097